PRAISE FOR *EVERYTHING MIND* BY CHRIS GROSSO

"I dig this book. By sharing his life's journey, Chris Grosso shines a light on our own. *Everything Mind* is a spiritual meal cooked for today, for us living now to taste, for our hearts and minds to digest." **JEFF BRIDGES**
Academy Award®-winning actor, musician, and *New York Times* bestselling coauthor of *The Dude and the Zen Master*

"If I begin to worry about the future of the Dharma Large—universal truth, genuinely enlightening practices, and the timeless wisdom traditions in our scientific, postmodern, secular era—I look to the younger generation for inspiration, people like fellow inter-meditator and Dharma buddy Chris Grosso. In *Everything Mind*, Backyard Bodhisattva Chris helps us make significant steps to recover from the human condition (of dissatisfaction and malaise) while juicing enticing ancient sutras, the Bible, the Vedas, and Zen koans. He combines this with the contemporary—thrash metal, skateboarding, and the Occupy movement—and the result is both sublime and delightful. His bullshit detector is well-tuned as he tears down spiritual barriers and constructs connections across generations, opening our inclusive everything minds *and* our spacious and warm everything hearts. This young Bodhisattva knows of what he speaks." **LAMA SURYA DAS**
author of *Make Me One with Everything* and *Awakening the Buddha Within,* and founder of the Dzogchen Center and Dzogchen Retreats

"Chris Grosso's *Everything Mind* will leave you rocking out to head-banger music, laughing until you pee, wishing you had finally gotten that tattoo, and in awe of the author's candid vulnerability as he shares tales of his audacious life. Because it slides down like a margarita on a hot summer night, you might not realize you've just had surgery. *Everything Mind* is a scalpel of truth, slicing through your illusions, your self-deceptions, your ego, and everything else that separates you from the magnificence of your spiritual essence. But fear not! This is a surgery you'll be grateful to undergo because it transports you into the frequency of miracles. This book will lay bare your soul and leave you breathless, your heart bursting open at the realization that we are all connected, we are perfect just as we are, we are never, ever alone, and if we're brave enough to walk the spiritual path with earnest humility, we can experience heaven on earth. Truly medicine for the soul. I love, love, love this book."

LISSA RANKIN, MD
New York Times bestselling author of *Mind Over Medicine* and *The Fear Cure*

"Chris Grosso's tough life lessons inform his no-bullshit spirituality in *Everything Mind*. A holy ferocity is in the heart of awakening; Chris takes us there and shares visionary tools to deepen with. Enter your true identity and wrestle with the tough questions as you enter *Everything Mind*." ALEX GREY
artist and cofounder of CoSM, Chapel of Sacred Mirrors

"*Everything Mind* offers heavyweight wisdom that's been tattooed with the mess and magnificence of life. In other words, it's a book about spirituality you can thoroughly trust because the gutsy author, Chris Grosso, ain't interested in hiding his humanity—he walks his talk with zero pretensions, raging authenticity, belly-shaking humor, breathtaking insight, a hellu-valotta honesty, and most inspiring of all, an Everything Heart. Read Grosso's rare book and experience the inimitable power of Keeping It Real."

SERA BEAK

author of *Red Hot and Holy*

"*Everything Mind* is just that—simultaneously expansive and intimate. Chris includes all aspects of life in his practice and his writing, and the result is a full picture of our shared human potential, for darkness, beauty, and freedom from suffering."

SHARON SALZBERG

cofounder of The Insight Meditation Society
and author of *Real Happiness*

"*Everything Mind* is a handy survival guide for the overgrown wilderness of contemporary consciousness and modern spiri-tuality. No map is the territory, and each of us has within us uncharted thoroughfares ready to be explored with fearless-yet-gentle analysis. Through a carefully curated and easily absorbed selection of quintessential quotes, intimate reflections, and pedestrian teachings—from the holiest of holies to the lowliest of lowlies—Chris helps us to help ourselves with practical exer-cises intended to identify, and softly unpack, anything in our personal baggage that isn't serving us on the trail, and thus pre-vents us from serving others. From wherever you are to wherever you're going, *Everything Mind* lays out flexible formulas, which will inevitably leave our campsites of the mind a little better than we found them."

LIAM WILSON

musician (The Dillinger Escape Plan)

"Chris Grosso speaks in a voice that is both sublime and grounded. He manages to convey the luminous essence of the perennial wisdom traditions with a deft and relevant touch that makes this essence—what Chris calls 'Everything Mind'—accessible to the beginner and fresh for those who have walked the path for long enough to have become cynical. Hilarious, skillful, authoritative, and humble, *Everything Mind* will help readers cultivate contemplative awareness and compassion in action. This book made me smile with irreverent delight and ache with longing for that which transcends all form and yet is embodied at the heart of the human experience. I'm so excited by this work and am grateful for Chris in this world."   **MIRABAI STARR**

author of *God of Love* and *Caravan of No Despair*

"If you are drawn to how real humans—with all the messiness of depression and addiction, anger and self-hatred—can walk an authentic spiritual path, please read *Everything Mind*. Chris Grosso, in telling his story, inspires us to find within our own imperfect selves the very source of love and freedom."

TARA BRACH, PHD

author of *Radical Acceptance* and *True Refuge*

"There is great difficulty afoot on any spiritual path. There is also strangeness, each of us approaching it in our own unique way. With *Everything Mind*, Chris Grosso empowers us to continue our quest no matter how difficult and strange it may be. I have already found the book to be a validating force on my own path. Take a day out of your life and read Chris Grosso's book, *Everything Mind*. You will find a wealth of knowledge, inspiration, and the most down-to-earth explanation of spiritual concepts that I've yet seen."   **TOMMY ROSEN**

yoga teacher and author of *Recovery 2.0*

"Chris manifests his 'indie spirituality' by drawing upon and finding the connections between spiritual traditions from the East and West and shining a whole new light on them to reveal a fresh relevance. He can segue from Foo Fighters to Thich Nhat Hanh to Charles Bukowski and have it make sense. This book is the immense heart—Chris Grosso shows up on every page with so much love, generosity of spirit, and compassion for the reader and his subject matter that you can't help but connect with him in his remarkable Everything Mind. This is a valuable friend to have on the path." **STEPHEN AND ONDREA LEVINE**
bestselling authors of *Embracing the Beloved,*
Who Dies? and *The Grief Process*

"Chris Grosso is an honest and engaging young teacher, and his work is both clearly expressed and inspiring."
ANDREW HARVEY
bestselling author of *The Hope*

"Spirituality is formless, yet it evolves with every new experience—and it is from each of these experiences in life that we learn. Chris Grosso adds to this evolution with ruthless honesty in a loving deposition that shares his experiences along the path of his own personal transformation. *Everything Mind* is a reflection of life." **DON MIGUEL RUIZ JR.**
bestselling author of *The Five Levels of Attachment*

"*Everything Mind* came to me in the middle of a personal spiritual trial. It is pure and simple wisdom born from a true heart and clear mind. Chris Grosso speaks to my soul."
SCOTT KELLY
musician (Neurosis, Tribes of Neurot, Shrinebuilder, Corrections House, Scott Kelly and the Road Home)

"In this age where there are so many distractions from career, family, and relationships, we often do not spend enough time checking in on ourselves and understanding how to tap into the inner peace within. Hence we experience stress, anger, depression, anxiety, and all other afflictive emotions. In *Everything Mind*, Chris Grosso offers pragmatic methods to address these afflictive emotions. He explains clearly how compassion and wisdom, first to oneself and later expanding it to include everyone else, are universal methods of achieving inner peace and healing which transcend society-defined labels of religion, culture, and race."

TSEM RINPOCHE
author of *Compassion Conquers All*

"Partly autobiographical, partly a manual for awakening and healing, *Everything Mind* will change you. Chris Grosso's special gift is his ability to translate complex spiritual teachings into vignettes that give us a sense of what an awakened life looks like. His words give us courage to look at our lives without judgment and adopt a practice that can turn our troubles into gifts that bring us into compassion and wisdom. *Everything Mind* will inspire you to engage with your pain, reclaim your passion for change, and in the process discover the truth of your life." **ADAM BUCKO**
coauthor of *Occupy Spirituality* and *The New Monasticism*

"*Everything Mind* is awesome! Chris understands the fundamental truth that it doesn't matter how different we think we are because deep down, we're all the same. Whether you're spiritual, religious, tattooed, a punk rocker, or simply seeking an alternative approach to exploring many of life's timeless inquiries, this book will be of great benefit to you. Super rad." **MIGUEL CHEN**
musician (Teenage Bottlerocket)

"*Everything Mind* offers us a deep, open-minded and inclusive look at what spiritual awakening is and how to integrate transformative practices into our real lives. Chris Grosso is a spiritual revolutionary. I am happy to have him as comrade in the struggle against greed, hatred, and ignorance. Read this book and join us in the coup d'état."   NOAH LEVINE
bestselling author of *Dharma Punx* and *Refuge Recovery*

"Chris Grosso's message of authenticity brings you to a place of truth and awareness, beyond the chaos of the current state of our everyday world. Another great masterpiece by a real modern-day guru, The Indie Spiritualist."   DON JOSE RUIZ
New York Times bestselling coauthor of *The Fifth Agreement*

EVERYTHING MIND

Also by Chris Grosso

Indie Spiritualist: A No Bullshit Exploration of Spirituality

EVERYTHING MIND

what i've learned about hard knocks,
spiritual awakening, and the
mind-blowing truth of it all

CHRIS GROSSO

WITHDRAWN

SOUNDS TRUE
BOULDER, COLORADO

Sounds True
Boulder, CO 80306

Published 2015

Cover design by Jennifer Miles
Book design by Beth Skelley

Kabir, *Kabir: Ecstatic Poems,* translated by Robert Bly. Used by permission of Beacon Press.
Heart Sutra, from *Zen Mountain Monastery Liturgy Manual,* by John Daido Loori. Used by permission of Zen Mountain Monastery.
Excerpt of eight lines from "the bluebird" from *The Last Night of the Earth Poems* by Charles Bukowski. Copyright © 1992 by Charles Bukowski. Reprinted by permission of HarperCollins Publishers.

Printed in the United States of America

Library of Congress Cataloging-in-Publication Data
Grosso, Chris.
  Everything mind : what I learned about hard knocks, spiritual awakening, and the mind-blowing truth of it all / Chris Grosso.
    pages cm
  Includes bibliographical references and index.
  ISBN 978-1-62203-529-8
  1. Spirituality. 2. Spiritual life. I. Title.
  BL624.G7663 2015
  204—dc23

                              2015004642

Ebook ISBN 978-1-62203-561-8

10 9 8 7 6 5 4 3 2 1

For Jenn and Morgan—my loves, my light, my grace

And for Abby, Onyx, Bentley, Sam, Mocha, Bowser,
Diesel, Toby, Mae, Snowball, and Curious.
Thank you for teaching me the true meaning
of unconditional love and acceptance.

CONTENTS

Chris Grosso's *Everything Mind* is a raw, real, authentic look at what is traditionally known as Enlightenment or Awakening or the Great Liberation—the discovery that we have an identity not just with a small, separate, finite self or mind (what Alan Watts called "the skin-encapsulated ego"), but also with a radically whole, infinite, all-embracing, and all-encompassing self or mind known as Buddha Mind, Christ Consciousness, Purusha, or Big Mind. Chris very appropriately calls this Everything Mind. "Everything" because, unlike the small mind or self, which identifies basically with just the "skin-encapsulated ego," Big Mind or Everything Mind identifies with *everything*—the entire manifest and unmanifest universe, the Ground of all Being, Godhead, the Kosmos, Buddha-nature, Brahman. Call it what you will, it is what there is and all there is. As the Upanishads famously put it, *tat tvam asi:* You Are That.

This might sound far-out and woo-woo, except that thousands and thousands of people over at least two millennia have had this direct and immediate experience of Enlightenment or Awakening, and their collective testimony is consistent, compelling, and altogether believable. What's more, you can directly and immediately have this experience for yourself and find out whether you believe it is true or not. Most people—educated or uneducated, rich or poor, brilliant or average—who have had a strong Enlightenment experience claim that, as one recently told me, "It was the most real reality I have ever known." The world's Great Religions were founded by men and women who originally had one of these Awakening experiences, realized that it had put them in touch with a Divine or Ultimate Reality, and set out to share that realization with others. There are traditions and practices and exercises that still exist today that can put you directly in touch with this all-pervading, all-embracing Everything Mind—and Chris's book is loaded with examples drawn from those that he has tried himself and found to be most valuable. He sets these forth in a clear, straightforward, no-nonsense fashion, which he elucidates with his trademark raw, authentic, and brutal honesty. This is indeed a no-bullshit spirituality, from one who has gone from gutter to glory, from ravaging drug addiction to the process of Awakening, from a living hell to a radiant heaven here and now. One thing is sure: as you read Chris's words, you can believe him. There are no lies in his narrative lines. He's seen where lies lead; he's been there, done that, and is now *done* with that, leaving only raw truth bleeding from a vulnerable, open heart.

If you look around the world of self-improvement or self-transformation, you notice that there are three main paths offered by various schools around the world. There is the path of Waking Up offered by the schools of the Great Liberation and aiming for Enlightenment or Awakening. There is the path of Cleaning Up, which aims to re-own and re-integrate previously repressed and dissociated shadow material, helping ameliorate any neuroses. And there is the path of Growing Up, the major stages of growth and development that all our multiple intelligences go through as they move from their earliest, immature, and undifferentiated forms to their highest, most mature, most differentiated and integrated forms (in other words, what happens as we actually "grow up" in any of our capacities). Chris stresses the first two—Waking Up to Everything Mind and Cleaning Up our shadow elements. He doesn't directly address Growing Up, but it is implicit in virtually all his recommendations, so let me say a few words about this so you can better understand where Chris is coming from, and because it is important that all three paths be engaged simultaneously, otherwise the result will turn out to be partial, fragmented, broken, tormented.

The path of Waking Up is a series of direct and immediate experiences that you are fully aware of as they happen. If you feel, for example, a loving oneness with the entire universe, you will know it—believe me. The stages in the path of Growing Up are not like that. You can't see them by introspecting. They are more like the rules of grammar. Everyone who grows up in a particular culture ends up speaking that language more or less correctly—they follow the rules of grammar. Yet, if you ask any of them to actually write down the rules they are following, very few can do so. In other words, they are following a large set of explicit rules but have no idea how they are doing it, let alone what those rules actually are. They can't see these rules by introspecting.

The stages in the path of Growing Up are like those rules of grammar. They are hidden values, meanings, needs, motivations, understandings, ethics and morals, worldviews—and they govern how we see and interpret our universe. They are not discovered by looking within, but by observing and interacting with many people over time. (In fact, they are so difficult to spot that, unlike the direct experiences of Waking Up—which go back at least fifty thousand years to the earliest shamans—the rules of the stages of Growing Up were only discovered about one hundred years ago.)

The way you do this is similar to the way American psychologist Lawrence Kohlberg explicated some of the major stages of our moral development (our moral Growing Up). You start by asking a series of questions—one of Kohlberg's most famous was, "A man is married to a woman who is dying of a particular illness. The local drugstore has a drug that will cure her, but he is very poor and cannot afford it. Does he have the right to steal it?" Kohlberg received three basic answers to this question: "Yes," "No," and "Yes."

When he asked the reason for the first "Yes" answer (why the husband had the right to steal the medicine), the person would answer with something like, "Well, what's right is whatever I say is right, whatever I want, and if I want to steal it, I'll steal it." This stage is variously called *egocentric, narcissistic, preconventional,* and *selfish.* It looks after itself, and only itself; it cares for itself, and only for itself. It is where all humans begin their growth and development to higher, wider, deeper stages of identity and capacity as they follow the path of Growing Up.

The "No" reason was, "What society says is true and its laws cannot be broken at all, so nobody has the right to steal this." This stage—which is more complex and more developed than the previous egocentric "Yes" stage—is known as: *ethnocentric* (extending identity from the individual self to a particular—"ethnic"—group or groups of people—a clan, tribe, race, sex, nation, religion, and so on; *care* (extending care from oneself to caring for an entire group—but just that one group, seeing everybody else as an outsider or other who doesn't deserve care); or *conventional* or *conformist.* The thought process at this stage is mythic and fundamentalist, with a strong "law and order" tendency and beliefs like "My country, right or wrong," or "My religion, right or wrong." In terms of spirituality, somebody at this growth stage will believe, for example, that all the myths in the Bible are literally true, that Moses really did part the Red Sea, God really did rain locusts down on the Egyptians, Christ really was born from a biological virgin, and so on.

The final "Yes" reason was, "He has the right to steal it because life is a universal value and worth more than the forty dollars that the medicine costs." This highest stage, based on universal principles that are true for all humans regardless of race, color, sex, or creed, is known as *worldcentric, rational, post-conventional, global, planetary.* It seeks fair treatment not just for individuals or their chosen group, but for all human beings. Odd as it sounds, this stance only showed up on the human scene around four hundred years ago. Before that, every known societal type had ethnocentric elements—slavery is a good example—and never questioned morality, as it was assumed to be the state of nature. In a hundred-year period, roughly from 1770 to 1870, slavery was outlawed from every rational-industrial society on our planet, the first time in our million-year history that anything like that had ever occurred.

If we look at ethicist and psychologist Carol Gilligan's stages of moral development in women, we find what she calls *selfish* (egocentric), *care* (ethnocentric), *universal care* (worldcentric), and finally *integrated* (an integral and wholistic inclusiveness). These stages are just a shortened version of the major stages that virtually all developmental researchers have found humans go through in their process of Growing Up in any of their intelligences or capacities.

The reason this is particularly important is that recent research has demonstrated that we can be at virtually any of those stages of Growing Up and have a major experience of Waking Up. However, when we do so, we interpret our Waking Up or Enlightenment experience according to our stage of Growing Up. If we are at a mythic ethnocentric stage, we will interpret our unity consciousness or Everything Mind according to the fundamentalist beliefs of that stage. If I am Christian at an ethnocentric stage of Growing Up and have an experience of unity consciousness or

Waking Up, I will indeed feel a profound unity with the entire world of Form—with *Everything*—but that is Form only as far as it is understood within that ethnocentric level. The higher levels of worldcentric and integral will be, as developmental psychologist Robert Kegan puts it, "over my head." Those higher levels haven't emerged in my case, and I obviously cannot be one with, or in unity with, something that doesn't even exist for me. Therefore, I will interpret my unity experience in ways that are deeply ethnocentric—such as sexist, racist, homophobic, highly authoritarian, or rigidly hierarchical, and always deeply fundamentalist. I will interpret those ethnocentric qualities as being part of ultimate reality, so of course I'll view slavery as okay, and of course homophobia as a correct stance, and of course sexism as part of Divinity—as almost every Great Religion espoused in its early, mythic, ethnocentric stages.

This ethnocentric Enlightenment is still common and widespread. For example, in *Zen at War,* Brian Daizen Victoria chronicles deeply and shockingly ethnocentric statements and actions by some of the most respected Zen masters in history. These types of ethnocentric statements occur in almost every spiritual tradition, simply because the stages of Growing Up, as I have pointed out, cannot be seen by introspecting, so they can't be reached by meditation or contemplation. Waking Up, *yes;* Growing Up, *no.* That's why not a single meditative or contemplative religion has anything resembling the major stages of Growing Up; and thus, while their exercises and practices do wonders for helping us Wake Up, they do nothing for helping us Grow Up. This must be addressed on its own, so that when we can have an experience of unity consciousness, or Everything Mind, we don't only Wake Up and Clean Up, we also have to Grow Up to our highest levels. This will lead to a genuine integration with all humans, indeed all reality, and not just with our "chosen people."

As you will find in *Everything Mind,* Chris has a deeply world-centric and integral orientation, and so he bends over backward to assure people that what is true for them is what is important; that all people be treated fairly and equally, regardless of race, color, sex, or creed (or appearance or clothing or language or practices). The sole thing he is consistently judgmental about—and entirely appropriately—is the fundamentalist stance, the belief that "I have the one and only true way," that "I have the only real approach to true God." What he's criticizing, of course, is this ethnocentricity, precisely because it represents a case of arrested development. He's acknowledging the higher stages of Growing Up that extend one's identity from just a particular group or single religion to a solidarity and care for all humans, for all sentient beings, and not just one particular "true" way.

Two thousand years ago, to include all perspectives was not a legitimate criticism or a basic concern. Rather, if you were Muslim, you defended Islam to the death (literally); if you were Christian, you defended Christianity to the death (literally); if you were Hindu, you defended Hinduism to the death (literally). It's only in the last four hundred years or so that this new level of moral Growing Up—that of global worldcentricity—has emerged, and thus a real concern for the importance and rights of the individual (and the universal rights of humans) has come to the fore. This is etched in Chris's own approach, which he calls indie spirituality, or spirituality focused on what the individual feels to be the most appropriate path, not what some tradition or dogma or outside authority claims is best. (Of course, we can take that too far. There are universal truths—including the very demand for universal tolerance and fairness—that are worldcentric, not just ethnocentric. I might believe fervently, in my heart of hearts, that 2 + 2 = 5, but that doesn't make it right; it is still a wrong belief, and it's wrong for everybody. The spiritual path of Waking Up is full of these kinds of universals, and we're not supposed to make them up ourselves, but see which ones resonate most, and then creatively build on those. But we do have to be careful here, especially with "following our own bliss"—because if that bliss is of the 2 + 2 = 5 variety, it's still wrong, no matter how deeply we feel it—and it will *never* lead to our true Awakening. This is especially a concern given the widespread legacy of the "me" generation. [If you'd like more information on the path of Growing Up, you might start with any book by Robert Kegan; in relation to spirituality, any book by James Fowler; or almost any of my books.])

Waking Up, Cleaning Up, Growing Up. Each of these is relatively independent. We can be highly advanced in one and poorly advanced in the others. A truly integral approach emphasizes and utilizes all three. Chris's whole approach is anchored in the higher reaches of Growing Up (worldcentric and integral), and from there, he gives a marvelous guide to the fundamentals of Waking Up, while also pointing out the crucial importance of Cleaning Up. He's a solid guide to our own growth and development along all three of these paths.

So, sit back and get ready for some raw, real, genuine, tried-and-true practices and explanations centering on our own deepest condition and reality, our universal, our Everything Mind. It's a trip—one you won't regret.

KEN WILBER

> You don't get explanations in real life.
> You just get moments that are absolutely,
> utterly, inexplicably odd.
>
> NEIL GAIMAN

INTRODUCTION

o here's the thing: I didn't go to school for any of this spirituality stuff. I'm not a yogi from the Himalayas, a preacher in a pulpit, or a "spiritual teacher" with dollar signs in my eyes. The truth is, early in life my curiosity got the better of me and led me down some roads that resulted in years of heavy drug and alcohol addiction. These dark places ultimately brought me to a very real life-or-death search for something more. That search is what this book is about: finding deeper meaning in life and waking up to the spiritual essence that imbues it all—from monasteries to stadiums, meditation to stage dives, skateboarding to serving food in a soup kitchen, and *everything* in between.

Wait . . . so by "everything," do I actually mean *every single thing?* Why, yes—yes, I do.

So, what is Everything Mind? Well, I think a better question would be, "What isn't Everything Mind?" We could start by saying that Everything Mind considers every-*thing* in our lives as part of the spiritual path. Our triumphs and heartbreaks, joys and suffering, the light and the dark—all are equally suitable teachers and lessons. Zen Buddhist teacher and poet Thich Nhat Hanh is famously quoted as saying, "No mud, no lotus," which means that our best selves grow out of our darkest places—our pain and suffering. Experiencing life from the place of Everything Mind allows us to lay aside our fears of right or wrong thoughts and emotions. Then, we can begin to compassionately, and even humorously (at times), work with and through *all* of them with open and courageous hearts and minds.

That's just the beginning. As we start to understand and engage our lives in a spiritual way, we realize that all that we *think* we are—our stories, hopes, experiences, fears, loves, and terrors—are just components of Everything Mind. This Everything Mind, this perfectly precise and inclusive stillness, holds each brilliant moment of who we are and who everyone is. It's like losing yourself so completely in your favorite song that *every-thing* else fades away, leaving you—intentionally or not—in a state of nonself. The song has penetrated your being so deeply that you forget about your material self—your thoughts, judgments, opinions, and labels—allowing that moment to simply be as it is. That's all there needs to be, and it's perfect.

The good news is, to begin awakening to Everything Mind, you don't have to be in a crisis of addiction (like I was), a religious scholar, or a renunciant. The tools for making positive changes and waking up to the deeper reality of life and of our human experience are, in this very moment, already inside of you. The celebrated, yet controversial, Buddhist teacher, poet, and artist Chögyam Trungpa Rinpoche once said, "Everything is a footprint of Buddha, anything that goes on, whether we regard it as sublime or ridiculous. Everything we do—breathing, farting, getting mosquito bites, having fantastic ideas about reality, thinking clever thoughts, flushing the toilet—whatever occurs is a footprint."[1] Looking through a Christian lens, the theologian and mystic Meister Eckhart wrote, "To be spiritual is to be awake and alive."[2] I believe it's important to note from the outset that being fully "awake and alive" isn't something we can learn from a book. So think of everything you read in these pages as nothing more than suggestions to guide you back within yourself to the place where the deeper truth of who you really are is already "awake and alive." This is the place where everything is a "footprint of Buddha"—the place of Everything Mind.

The S-Word. What Is Spirit?

Ah, Spirit. This can be a tricky discussion topic because Spirit has no ascertainable qualities; instead, it's more like an essence, something that is fluid and constantly evolving. On the physical level, I think of Spirit as manifesting from its boundless, formless essence into the many people, plants, mountains, oceans, microbes, atoms, and all the other incredible things that make up our consciousness, our Earth, and the entire wild and inspiring galaxy.

Author and philosopher Ken Wilber describes Spirit's evolution as *Spirit-in-action,* which means Spirit is perpetually awakening to more of Itself throughout each stage of Its evolution—from matter to body to mind to soul to Spirit—and with each unfolding, It becomes more aware of, and available to, Itself.

To further elaborate, in 1944, while giving a speech in Florence, Italy, the famed German theoretical physicist Max Planck said:

As a man who has devoted his whole life to the most
clear headed science, to the study of matter, I can tell
you as a result of my research about atoms this much:
There is no matter as such. All matter originates and
exists only by virtue of a force which brings the particle
of an atom to vibration and holds this most minute solar
system of the atom together. We must assume behind
this force the existence of a conscious and intelligent
mind. This mind is the matrix of all matter.[3]

For me, Plank's "force" represents Spirit. Right now, you may
be thinking to yourself, "Force? Spirit? Matrix of all matter? . . .
What?" I completely understand how some of this may sound a
bit weird, especially to those of you who are new to this wacky
world of spirituality. If you find that's the case, I encourage you
to take a few minutes (or as long as you need) to sit in contemplation of all this before you move on. Or, you can do what
I would most likely do: throw caution to the wind and forge
ahead, allowing things to unfold in their due course as you continue reading. Whatever works for you works for me.

Okay, So Then, What the Hell/Heaven Is Spirituality?

The beautiful thing is that if you ask ten different people what
spirituality means to them, you're likely to get ten different
answers, which makes it clear that spirituality truly is a highly
individualized process and experience. Nobody owns it—not
Buddhists or Hindus, Christians or Muslims, atheists or Jews.
The abridged definition I most often use is simply: *waking up.*
Spirituality is an interior journey, one that takes us beneath the
surface of who and what we think we are and guides each of us
home to our truest Self.

Spirituality emerges and grows from *our* individual experience of Spirit. That's one of the most important things I want to convey in this book: Find your own truth! I encourage you to become your own spiritual scientist. Be curious and, with an open heart and mind, explore what does—and does not—resonate for you on the spiritual path.

There are, of course, some pitfalls that can come with this path of direct connection. I'll address them in greater detail later, but briefly, here are two things to be aware of: when turning to your heart's guidance, watch out for any hidden, self-serving, or distorting motives; and don't allow your spiritual path to become one that is focused only on yourself and does not serve others in some way.

Exploration leads to practice—like spending more time in meditation, contemplation, or prayer, and a little (or a lot) less time on social media, or bringing more mindfulness (yes, I know *mindfulness* is a trendy spiritual word, but goddamn it, it's just so useful and convenient) to the activities we're passionate (and not so passionate) about. That's how we expand our perspectives. In doing so, we're also cultivating our inner knowing, wisdom, and intuition in a way that's directly experienced rather than hypothesized. It's in this authentic place that we uncover *our truth*—again, whatever that is for you—which is what matters most. I can never know what is happening inside of you—your thoughts, emotions, hopes, dreams, fears—so how could I, or anyone else, ever know what is and isn't spiritual for you, and vice versa? It's impossible. So, take an honest look inside and see, or, more accurately, *feel,* what is real for you, and then honor that, but try to do so with an inquisitive attitude, one that acknowledges that everything in life is subject to change (including our ideas, understandings, and experiences). There is *always* room for growth in our spiritual development, so do your best to stay open and fluid rather than closed and concrete as you progress on your path. Perhaps most traditionally "spiritual" things won't resonate for you, and that's fine. Spirituality *is not* found only in designated places at designated times. Spirituality *is* and *means* whatever it *is* and *means* for you—but keep in mind that even *spirituality* itself is just a word.

For me, besides it being just a word, spirituality is about waking up to the deeper dimensions of life that lie beneath our daily experiences—those dimensions that are filtered through our senses. Third-century Buddhist philosopher and founder of the Madhyamaka school of Mahāyāna Buddhism, Nāgārjuna, taught what's called the Two Truths doctrine—that form simultaneously coexists with formlessness, and that it's thanks to this formlessness that form can even exist in the first place. The beauty of the Two Truths is that it gives expression to nondual truth, something I'll explore in greater detail later on. But for now, just know that the Transformers theme song was really onto something when it said, "More than meets the eye." (Not to downplay the importance of the Autobots waging battle to destroy the evil forces of the Decepticons, because that was some important shit too, but covering their ongoing saga is beyond the scope of this book.)

Other people are going to have different ideas, experiences, and definitions of spirituality, and that's great. For example, a while back I interviewed Zach Lind, drummer for the band Jimmy Eat World. Knowing he was a Christian (who doesn't allow himself to get wrapped up in the dogma), I asked him how he honored his faith and incorporated the Bible and scripture into his life despite the particularly unpopular or anachronistic elements in there like homophobia, violence, and sexism. Zach answered:

As a Christian, I feel that the Bible is important, but I also feel it's often misused. I like to allow my direct experience to be guided and inspired by what scripture says, but if there's something written that's different from what my own experience is telling me, I honor my experience. Like, for example, of course I believe it's okay for women to speak in church and to teach men, because my experience with women in my life—my wife, my mom, and my female friends—is one that tells me they can obviously teach and lead. So, I don't need to base my ideas of gender roles, especially in relation to the Church, on a text that's thousands of years old.[4]

As Zach exemplifies, spirituality, and even religion, is not a zero-sum game. It's about experience. It's about peeling away the layers of our unexamined beliefs, identities, and dogmas rather than adding to them. It's about waking up to deeper truths of who and what we are and what the hell is actually going on in this thing we call life. Thank God there are a number of different ways, paths, and teachings to help us do just that, many of which I'll explore throughout this book, but again, I can't stress enough the importance of you trying them out for yourself and finding the means and ways that are right *for you*.

Many people who may not consider themselves "spiritual" are essentially living a "spiritual" lifestyle (again, remembering that spirituality is just a word). It's in keeping ourselves open to others that we're available to receive wisdom teachings at all times. For example, my friend Chris Stedman is an atheist. He's also the humanist chaplain at Yale University, and author of the book *Faithiest: How an Atheist Found Common Ground with the Religious*. (*Faithiest* is a derogatory term used by some atheists to describe other atheists who respect and are open to dialogue with religious people.) Chris wouldn't necessarily call himself spiritual; however, I'd say he's one of the most heart-centered and spiritual people I've ever met. In *Faithiest,* he wrote:

> The truth I aim to communicate is a simple and universal one: that all folks, whether Muslim or Christian or Hindu or atheist, deserve equal dignity. I hope my story will illuminate the problems that arise when we dehumanize people because of their atheism or religiosity, and when we resort to negative rhetoric and name calling instead of seeking to understand our differences.
>
> Just as I've personally reclaimed "queer" from those who have used it in an attempt to discount the legitimacy of my identity, I now reclaim "faithiest." If such a label insinuates that I am interested in both exploring godless ethics and identifying and engaging shared values with the religious—in putting "faith" in my fellow human beings and our shared potential to overcome the false dichotomies that keep us apart—then I am all for it.[5]

For me, this is as fine an example of spirituality as any other I've come across. Living a compassionate and heart-centered life, one that also seeks to benefit other beings, is spiritual, regardless of whether you choose to call it that or not. A lot of people get caught up in the semantics and have heavy associations around certain words, like "God," and "spirituality," but I don't. In the interest of full disclosure, here's a heads up: I do use words like *spirituality* and *God* and *sacred* throughout this book, but never with a dogmatic or authoritarian intent. When you read the word *God* here, it could just as easily be replaced with *ISness,*

Being, Suchness, Stillness, Emptiness—Everything Mind—and still have the same meaning.

To again quote the brilliant Meister Eckhart, "I pray God to rid me of God," by which I believe he meant: may all concepts about God be removed so She or He or It can be directly experienced as a living reality. Eckhart further elaborated on this when he wrote, "Love God as God is—a not-God, not-mind, not-person, not-image—even more, as he is a pure, clear One, separate from all twoness."[6] To break that down, Eckhart is saying that God is in every single thing, just as every single thing is in God, because God is "separate from all twoness," which can also be understood as panentheism.

This is reminiscent of the Buddhist concept of *śūnyatā,* which states that no person or thing exists on its own, so everything is empty of an individual and permanent self—separate from all twoness. So let's just say that, whether we like it or not, God is completely unavoidable. On the other hand, if you prefer, you can give it another name and just throw the entire notion of God out the window and focus on the rest of the material in this book. I'm equally cool with whichever way you decide to go on that.

Why Spirituality?

It's not like spirituality is going to magically fix everything. In some cases it can make things seem worse and more chaotic before they get better. If we're being totally real about our practice, spirituality will inevitably, at some point, shake and crumble the carefully crafted foundations of what we believe about ourselves, others, and life in general. This is because spirituality dismantles all the conditioning we've been subject to since birth, be it from our family, friends, teachers, or society as a whole. Raw spirituality, rather than adding more beliefs and ideas about who and what we think we are, peels them away, bringing us deeper within ourselves to the place where the realest of real truths resides—another topic I'll come back to later.

I know the entire previous section hammered home the fact that spirituality is just a word, and thus, whatever we make of it, *it is*. However, I also think it's worth mentioning that when I talk about spirituality, I mean it as something that's raw and direct. It's not just about creeds or beliefs, but rather about being directly of the heart and the mind in a way that's undeniable. That is why cultivating a spiritual lifestyle might be one of the most challenging undertakings you'll ever face.

Things such as learning to live mindfully (that damn word again) with the acceptance of whatever life hands us, seeing (and honoring) the beauty, wonder, and interconnectedness of all things (and I mean *all* things—remember that mud and that lotus), and cultivating a greater sense of loving-kindness for ourselves as well as others definitely won't always be the blissed-out love-and-light endeavor that many think spirituality is supposed to be.

So, *why* spirituality? Why not? Many of us have sought happiness in things like food, drugs, shopping, sex, and TV, only to realize that what they offer is nothing more than fleeting satisfaction. Hey, I love to zone out and watch *The Walking Dead* as much as the next guy, but once that hour of zombierific goodness is over, it's over, and then what? That new car, laptop, or guitar that makes us so happy when we buy it—the one that we're extra careful not to get any scratches or scuff marks on—usually loses its appeal not too long after we've acquired it. Once the nicks and dings begin to appear (and they always do), we're on to the next thing.

Of course it's fine to enjoy the material things in life, but it's important to do so with the understanding that none of them will ever provide us with a lasting source of peace, happiness, or contentment. Learning to live mindfully (okay, I just give up), with a heart that is open to all life—its pain and pleasures, ups and downs—as cultivated through various spiritual practices, is how we come to know real peace, happiness, and contentment.

In the foreword to Chögyam Trungpa Rinpoche's classic book *Cutting Through Spiritual Materialism,* his son and Tibetan Buddhist teacher Sakyong Mipham Rinpoche wrote, "Spiritual awakening is not a happy-go-lucky endeavor. The path of truth is profound—and so are the obstacles and possibilities for self-deception."[7] So again, spirituality is not a quick fix that magically makes life amazing. However, it can teach us to make ourselves available to life, accepting whatever we face with an open heart and working through it with skillful means.

After we spend some time working with spiritual practices and learning from those who've walked the path before us, it's inevitable that we will begin to awaken in new ways. So if you're up for a wondrous, strange, beautiful, eye-popping, and mind-melting experience, one that is simultaneously nothing special at all, then I'd say you're very much ready to open your Everything Mind.

Bringing Darkness to Light

It's fair to say that our natural tendency as humans is to avoid pain and discomfort at virtually all costs. However, when we do this, we keep ourselves locked in a perpetual cycle of more of the same—more pain; more dis-ease; more sadness, hurt, anger, and fear. Buddhist nun Pema Chödrön once said, "When we protect ourselves so we won't feel pain, that protection becomes like armor, like armor that imprisons the softness of the heart."[8] And so it's through cultivating compassion, rather than aversion, for our pain, our addictions, and our lives that we're now bringing *everything* to the path, remembering that both the light and the dark are a part of Everything Mind, not just the things that make us comfortable. With this acceptance, we're free to embrace life's struggles with the softness of our hearts and begin to sincerely heal from the inner wounds that we've spent much of our lives trying to avoid.

The greatest sources of hurt and emotional wounds in my life are the result of many years of drug addiction, and some of the experiences I've written about in this book are directly related to those. But I'd like to share a quick story to help illustrate that, whether or not you've ever suffered from drug and alcohol addiction, chances are you're in recovery from something—being bullied as a child, sexual abuse, depression, or anxiety, to name just a few.

Several years ago, when I interviewed the wonderful Trappist monk Father Thomas Keating, I mentioned to him that I was in recovery from drug addiction. To this day, I remember his words as if he spoke them to me only a moment ago. While laughing a playful and gentle laugh, he said, "I'm in recovery too, but from the human condition and the addictive process that we all seem to suffer from in varying degrees of severity."[9] How true is that? It's like the Buddha said in his first truth, which is one of the fundamental teachings of Buddhism: if you've taken a human birth, you're inevitably going to experience pain and suffering (or unsatisfactory-ness) in life. *But* . . . as the Buddha went on to teach, the degree to which we suffer is much more within our control than we think, which is yet another topic we'll delve into later on. So, throughout this book, any time I write about addiction, please take it as an opportunity to shine a light on your own challenges and your own recovery.

Why Listen to Me?

Okay, I have to put on my really serious face to answer this question, otherwise I'd go off on some sarcastic tangent that would probably have *too much* fun with the whole "sales pitch" thing. (My editors have emphasized that I really need to connect with you here as I finish the introduction, dear reader, in a way that establishes trust and builds a rapport. So here goes. . . .) We've all been through our share of shit in life. My journey happened to take me down some roads that were darker than many (though not as dark as others). Considering the way I lived for many years, it truly is a miracle that I'm alive today. The addiction, jails, suicide attempts, rehabs, detoxes, emergency rooms, and psychiatric hospitals that I wrote candidly about in my first book, *Indie Spiritualist,* were my reality for years. But now, I am free from all those things. Not only that, but today I actually enjoy life, which is something that in the depths of my complete and utter brokenness, I never thought I would be able to say. So if I can go from living a life of complete hopelessness and despair to one with noticeably more contentment, gratitude, and joy, I absolutely believe you can too. There is always hope.

What I offer in this book are my candid experiences of the life-changing (and -saving) lessons that I learned (and continue to learn) on my spiritual journey. I am where I am today because of what I've learned from many of the great wisdom traditions (including Buddhism, Advaita Vedanta, Christian mysticism, and Taoism) that have guided me along the way, and because I've brought those teachings and experiences into my everyday life—skateboarding; enjoying hip-hop and hardcore; being a loving husband, father, and son; and so much more. It's *all* relevant in Everything Mind.

In the pages that follow, I want to give you my insides—unfiltered and undiluted. Along with this raw offering come—and in complete clarity, I might add—my imperfections. I write from this place of vulnerability because I want you to see me in all my humanity—*all of it.* I am a real person who would never pretend I have all the answers or this life thing entirely figured out. I don't. On top of that, I have no shortage of flaws, though I do try my best to be a little better each day, and I think there's something to be said for that. It's important for me to be real with you about this because I hope it encourages you to be real with yourself while doing whatever you need to in order to be a little better each day as well. So please, find your own answers and have your own experiences, because it's that—and only that—which will lead you to the truth. And as we all know, it's the truth that will set us free from fear and unnecessary suffering.

Maybe your idea of Spirit and spirituality will be different from mine, and maybe it won't; either way, it doesn't matter. What *does* matter is that our experiences are genuine, authentic, and illuminating for *each of us,* reminding us of who we are at the ultimate depth of our being, the furthest reaches of our Everything Mind. It truly is nothing short of fucking fantastic, I assure you. (Okay, that wasn't so bad. Thanks, editors.)

Once the seed of awakening
sprouts in you, there's no choice—
there's no turning back.

RAM DASS

1

THE GODDAMN RED PILL

There's really no way to dance around this: once you step onto the spiritual path, as Ram Dass says, there's no turning back. You can certainly decide anytime you'd like that this spirituality thing isn't for you, but you should know that our existence as sentient beings is one of Spirit-in-action, which means Spirit is continually awakening to more of Itself through the manifest world of form. Once you begin to explore Everything Mind and awaken to that connection with Spirit, game on.

Consider yourself warned. If you're going to turn back, "Turn back now" (spoken in a creepy old-man voice from a 1980s horror movie, of course), for this spirituality thing will later be nothing less than a nagging pain in the ass if you try to call it quits. The reason? Well, it's like this: Have you ever been making out with someone and things are getting (oh God, I'll be cliché and say it) hot and heavy, and right before things end up where you're hoping they will, the other person decides to stop? Man, how that sucks. (Not that I would know personally or anything, but so I've heard.) That example really isn't far off from what our relationship with Spirit and awakening is actually like.

Spirit wants us to "get off" (well, in a sense) as It merges with us in a way that we remember It as our true Self. Held in that remembrance is not only the experience of the absolute perfection that we truly are, but also the key to liberating ourselves from so much unnecessary pain and suffering.

Of course, Spirit wants to "get off" too, but the only way It can is by continuing to awaken to Itself through you, and through me, and through all sentient beings. So yes, you're free to walk away from the spiritual path anytime you'd like, but just know that, simply because you stepped away, Spirit isn't going anywhere. Be prepared to experience frequent (and often annoying) bouts of internal yearning from Spirit calling you back home (very much in the same way that the addict who has a taste of sobriety can never go back to using and enjoy it in the same way again). The call may be gentle, or, as in my case, more like getting hit over the head with a brick, but one way or another, the call is inevitably (and persistently) going to be there.

Not too long ago, I found myself contemplating the whole spiritual-path thing after a relatively harmless incident I witnessed at a stoplight. It couldn't have been more than two seconds from the time the light turned from red to green when all of a sudden an extremely agitated driver in a Jeep the next lane over yelled, "It's a green light, asshole!" at the woman in front of him. He obviously startled her, and she proceeded to dart off. And, while I felt bad for the poor lady, I couldn't help but laugh as I read the "Life Is Good" tire cover on the back of the pissed-off guy's Jeep as he drove away.

Later that day, I remembered that rageaholic—hey, Homer Simpson said it, so it's a word as far as I'm concerned—driver, and this, for whatever reason, led me a few moments later to thinking about the scene from the movie *The Matrix* where Morpheus offers Neo the red pill—you know, the one that if swallowed would show him "just how deep the rabbit hole goes." As I thought about that crossroads where Neo found himself, I related it to my own life and wondered, what if I had never set out on this spiritual adventure?

I considered how much easier things might have been if I didn't give a shit about others and lived from a completely selfish and reactionary place, acting impulsively on my emotions just like that pissed-off Jeep driver had. It was at this point that the reality of my situation set in, and I realized that, just like Neo after swallowing the red pill, once we've encountered Everything Mind, there is no forgetting it.

There was definitely a time in my life when I didn't give two shits about yelling at other drivers, or about other people's feelings at all—unless they were friends or family, and even then it wasn't all the time. But these days, things are different. I find that having traveled the spiritual path for awhile, I feel significantly less compelled to act out old behaviors like yelling at cars or holding anger in my heart toward others. (Damn you, mindfulness, and your subsequent sense of responsibility.)

Trust me, though; I'm no saint. (*Fuck, shit, balls.* There, point proven.) There are definitely still times when I'll catch myself acting out, but thanks to working with various traditional and nontraditional spiritual practices (many of which I share throughout this book), I've found it is so much easier and more natural to be kind to people—including myself.

Still, this process of opening our Everything Minds can be difficult and requires a lot of patience. Chögyam Trungpa Rinpoche broke it down for us like this:

My advice to you is not to undertake the spiritual path.
It is too difficult, too long, and is too demanding. . . .
I would suggest . . . you ask for your money back, and
go home now. . . . This is not a picnic. It is really going
to ask everything of you. . . . So, it is best not to begin.
However, if you do begin, it is best to finish.[1]

Now, I don't want to give anyone the wrong idea and say that embarking on the spiritual path is not worth it, because in my own experience, no matter how difficult it may be, it absolutely *is* worth it. I'm sure those of you reading this, who are walking the walk—be it the first nervous step or the last leg of the marathon—know exactly what I'm saying. But I'm also sure that you too can relate to how extremely tough it can be at times.

The great Sufi mystic Rumi writes, "Yesterday I was clever, so I wanted to change the world. Today I am wise, so I am changing myself."[2] We make these changes by taking little steps inward each day: we find the practices that are suitable for us, the ones that open our minds to the deeper meanings of life, the ones that show us how to lay our heart armor aside. As we do this, we connect to a deeper space of love and understanding within ourselves, one that all sentient beings share. The place Hindus refer to when greeting one another with *namaste*—"I see the Divine in you"—or meditators experience when all sense objects have fallen away and all that's left is a perfect, all-inclusive stillness. It's the place of Everything Mind.

So again dear reader, you've been warned. (*Mua-ha-ha-ha.*) To reemphasize Trungpa Rinpoche's words, "This is not a picnic. It is really going to ask everything of you." But the thing is, I truly believe that if you take into consideration the alternative, which is to say the humdrum dullness of a life lived grasping at external objects for fleeting happiness, it will be clear that there really never was much of a choice to begin with.

Within us—the flames of the end.

AT THE GATES, "UNDER A SERPENT SUN"

CALCULATING INFINITY

Have you ever had one of those experiences where you found yourself thinking, "Huh? I didn't see that coming." Yup, me too.

This particular one happened on a day that started like any other. But then, isn't that always the way? I woke up, meditated, read, and wrote a bit, caught up on some emails—the normal morning routine. Then I put on my bargain-bin running attire and got ready for my morning jog.

As soon as I stepped outside, I noticed that my surroundings seemed exceptionally beautiful that morning. It was a quintessential fall day in New England, complete with leaves changing color, soft white clouds scattered across a perfect blue sky, and a gentle breeze for good measure. This kind of beauty obviously needed a soundtrack, so I found no more suitable companion than that of Swedish metal band At the Gates on my iPod. It *was* October, and nothing says Halloween quite like metal, and Swedish metal at that—except of course for Norwegian black metal, but that's another conversation entirely.

I was roughly ten minutes into my run and making my way down one of the main roads in my rural town when something strange and beautiful happened. As I was running, I—Christ, how do I even word this? It was as if everything both exploded and imploded simultaneously in my consciousness, resulting in a completely abstract yet perfectly obvious sense of perfection. It was as if I was home—not the home where I lay my head at night, but you know, *home home.* I'd had some similar experiences in the past, but none that I recall being quite as powerful, and definitely none of this magnitude.

As I continued running, a euphoric, almost overwhelming feeling of rapture engulfed what I can only describe as my entire essence of being. (I'd say both inside and out, but there were no "inside" and "out" at this point.) It was an experience of . . . well . . . a nonexperience. However, there was a subtle yet absolute and complete perfection I was aware of along with just a tinge of awareness of tears streaming down my cheeks—so it wasn't *exactly* a nonexperience, but still, that is the closest I can come to putting words to it.

Before I take you any further on this woo-woo-sounding, esoteric journey, let me assure you, I'm not exaggerating any of this: I, a grown-ass man, was jogging down one of the main roads in a rural town with tears streaming from my eyes and a big-ass smile on my face. The experience was short-lived, though (lasting maybe a minute or so), as I found my awareness shifting from one of complete and full perfection back to a self-conscious sense of just how insane I must have looked to the oncoming motorists. That's all it took for me to sink back into my "normal" waking state.

In that euphoria, I experienced, well, everything—the unabridged totality of life. I really don't know how else to explain it, and I'm sure that might leave some of you scratching your heads, but it truly defied my rational mind. I still had a visual awareness of my surroundings, but everything else had faded away: my body, At the Gates, *everything,* leaving me with only a precise stillness, a stillness in which *everything* resided. *Everything Mind!*

And within that everything was you . . . I mean it: *you.* Not the physical you reading these words right now, but the conscious awareness that makes it possible for you to read these words in the first place; the You underneath the you. You were there with me, and together, we were in the vast place that gives birth to all things—both manifest and unseen.

The last thing I can really say about this is: if I had died in that moment, it would have been perfection personified, bringing me home . . . with You by my side.

Your mind constantly returns to
a place that's not so fucking cold,
but on fire with war.

PROPAGANDHI, "NIGHT LETTERS"

3

THE HOPE AND THE HURT

Sri Ramana Maharshi is one of the most celebrated and world-renowned Hindu masters of all time, and his teaching of self-inquiry is easily one of the most influential elements of my own path. He was born in 1879 near Madurai, Tamil Nadu, India, and, at the age of sixteen, had an experience that shattered the foundation of his sense of self, changing the course of both his life and, later, many of his devotees' lives forever. Regarding the experience, Ramana said:

> It was quite sudden. I was sitting in a room on the first floor of my uncle's house. I seldom had any sickness and on that day there was nothing wrong with my health, but a sudden, violent fear of death overtook me. There was nothing in my state of health to account

for it; and I did not try to account for it or to find out whether there was any reason for the fear. I just felt, "I am going to die," and began thinking what to do about it. It did not occur to me to consult a doctor or my elders or friends. I felt that I had to solve the problem myself, then and there.

The shock of the fear of death drove my mind inward and I said to myself mentally, without actually framing the words: "Now death has come; what does it mean? What is it that is dying? This body dies." And I at once dramatized the occurrence of death. I lay with my limbs stretched out stiff as though rigor mortis had set in and imitated a corpse so as to give greater reality to the enquiry. I held my breath and kept my lips tightly closed so that no sound could escape, so that neither the word "I" or any other word could be uttered. "Well then," I said to myself, "this body is dead. It will be carried stiff to the burning ground and there burnt and reduced to ashes. But with the death of this body am I dead? Is the body 'I'? It is silent and inert but I feel the full force of my personality and even the voice of the 'I' within me, apart from it. So I am Spirit transcending the body. The body dies but the Spirit that transcends it cannot be touched by death. This means I am the deathless Spirit."[1]

It's extremely rare for someone to become completely awakened or instantaneously self-actualized the way Sri Ramana was. For most of us, it takes time and sincere effort (which is an interesting dichotomy because everything we're searching for, or wanting to awaken to, is all already here anyway). That's usually not a very popular truth—that the spiritual process takes time—because we want what we want when we want it. Right? The desire for instant gratification is a hell of a thing, and having spent so much of my life in active addiction, I understand.

Ken Wilber, while not addressing the disease of addiction and recovery specifically, but rather spirituality in general (which I believe are intertwined anyway), laid it out so clearly for us when he wrote:

> Nobody will save you but you. You alone have to engage your own contemplative development. There is all sorts of help available, and all sorts of good agency to quicken this development, but nobody can do it for you. And if you do not engage this development, and on your deathbed you confess and scream out for help to God, nothing is going to happen. Spiritual development is not a matter of mere belief. It is a matter of actual, prolonged difficult growth, and merely professing belief is meaningless and without impact. It's like smoking for twenty years, then saying, "Sorry, I quit." That will not impress cancer. Reality, in other words, is not interested in your beliefs; it's interested in your actions, what you actually do, your actual karma.[2]

For me, the first step toward contemplative development was recovery. Let's face it, waking up in a jail cell with little to no recollection of how you got there really isn't anyone's idea of a good time—okay, at least it's not *most* people's idea of a good time. However, thanks to living in active addiction for many years, I've managed to accomplish this feat on more than a few occasions. I've knocked on death's door numerous times because of my addiction and have spent more time in detoxes, rehabs, psychiatric hospitals, and jails than I care to (or can) remember.

After using from the age of fifteen until I was thirty-three, I'm grateful to be sober today. This isn't my first time in recovery, but it's definitely the longest and most heart-centered attempt I've ever made. I attribute the better part of these years of recovery to something I'm grateful to have *finally* learned, something I'd let slip through my ears at 12-step meetings or while listening to various dharma talks for far too long. So I ask you to *please* hear me when I say that the healing process—which goes for both addicts and nonaddicts alike—is always, *always,* an inside job. Fuck—how I wish I'd let that sink in sooner.

My head was so far up my ass that I would actually believe that whenever I'd made it to around six months clean, and begun getting material things back in my life like a job, car, and apartment, that I was fine, I was cured. I had the warped idea that I was "recovering" because I was abstaining from drugs and alcohol. If I had money coming in through steady work, was somewhat accountable to people, had a girlfriend, and was on good terms with my family, then in my mind I was recovering . . . except the thing was, I wasn't, not even a little.

Sure, I was going to some 12-step meetings while also frequenting various meditation groups. I certainly talked the talk, but by keeping my "recovery" material-based and never cultivating the courage to look at and work with the real problem—the residual mental, emotional, and spiritual mess left inside of me—I was only prolonging the inevitable, which was picking up and using again.

Today, while recognizing that recovery is only a day-at-a-time reprieve, I've finally come to know better. Through the 12-step fellowships as well as various spiritual teachings and practices like meditation, mantra, and self-inquiry, I've learned that in order to heal, I have to fearlessly and intimately sift through the wreckage of my past—something that can be terribly scary, difficult, and entirely unpleasant. In order to have a fighting chance at saving my life, this is a decision that I have to make on a daily basis; and today, I choose life. I choose to be fearless in the face of adversity. (Please note: The 12-step fellowship and various spiritual practices and teachings mentioned throughout this book are simply what work for me. I encourage you to find whatever model works for you, whether it's yoga, refuge recovery, integral recovery, or whatever other means resonate for you and allow the healing to begin.)

I feel blessed to be a part of the miracle of recovery, a miracle that continues to unfold not only in my life but also in countless other lives everywhere. At the same time, the nightmare of addiction is still very much alive for many suffering addicts—and not only the addicts themselves, but their loved ones too, who can do little more than watch helplessly as the life of the person they love deteriorates.

In 12-step fellowships, there's a saying, "We do recover," which I love, because it's a beacon of hope for the hopeless. I remind myself of this sentiment quite often. At the same time, to say, "We die," would be just as accurate a statement. Morbid as it sounds, it's the reality of this disease. I've seen so many wonderful lives end before they'd been fully lived, and it's fucking heartbreaking; but to keep our recovery in order, we can't forget this sad truth, because if we do, we could be next.

A few years ago, on the day my first book was released, I received an email from a friend whom I hadn't spoken with in quite some time. We had gone our separate ways because we were both dealing with issues that made our relationship toxic. (That's the really neat and tidy version.) My friend's words really touched me, particularly the following:

> I just got home from an incredibly emotional experience. I stopped into the bookstore tonight to buy your

book. Johnny Cash was playing, and I nearly lost it when I found you in the stacks between *A Course in Miracles* and Ram Dass. I thought to myself, "I used to look through the obituaries for your name, and now I'm looking through the stacks in a major bookstore for you." My God, I don't have the words . . . I'm just so glad that you're well.

The sad thing is that she was totally justified in looking for my name in the obituaries because on any given day there was a very real chance she could have found it there. Reading my friend's words made me think back to the countless times I'd cried while holding a bottle of alcohol, or looking at a line of coke (or Ritalin) on a table, not wanting to drink or snort it but still doing so—a slave to a disease that was destroying me.

You may not be able to relate to any of this, but I would guess that, even if my specific experiences aren't yours, you still have your own emotional scars, your own painful memories. If so, I want you to know that you're not alone. There are many of us here with you, right now and in this very moment. We may not be physically present, but at the level of the heart, and in the place of Everything Mind—the place where we feel both the most excruciating pain and the most overwhelming love—we're right here, side by side.

There are times when I still feel guilty for having survived when so many others didn't. It's at those times, though, that I have to give myself a reality check and recognize that while yes, I've done some terribly shitty things in my life when under the influence, I've also been blessed with the opportunity to help others in their own process of recovery (and not just from addiction). For me, there's no greater gift than that—the chance to be of service and help others help themselves.

I hope anyone who's struggling with addiction, depression, self-loathing, or feelings of hopelessness finds some semblance of hope in my words, some way to engage their "contemplative development" or, at the very least, learns from my past mistakes and saves some time and pain in their own healing process . . . because we're all human, we're all recovering from something, and we've all hurt enough already, haven't we?

My heart has softened; my mind
has quieted down. These days, I rarely
want to bash anyone's head in.

NOAH LEVINE

4

BREATHE IN THE FIRE

Keeping our hearts open and vulnerable is one of the scariest and yet most transformative things we can do in our lives. While this may sound counterintuitive, when we keep our hearts open, touching the center of our pain and feeling it in a completely raw way, it helps us become clearer on the areas where we still have aversions and attachments—the real places where we still have work to do.

We spend so much unnecessary time suffering because we're not in touch with our hearts' emotional energy, intelligence, and guidance. Yes, I know it may sound corny, but it's very real. There's been some wonderful work done around this by the folks at HeartMath, and on the topic of heart intelligence they've said:

Heart intelligence is the flow of awareness, understanding and intuition we experience when the mind and emotions are brought into coherent alignment with the heart. It can be activated through self-initiated practice, and the more we pay attention when we sense the heart is speaking to us or guiding us, the greater our ability to access this intelligence and guidance more frequently. Heart intelligence underlies cellular organization and guides and evolves organisms toward increased order, awareness and coherence of their bodies' systems.[1]

The thing is, rather than paying attention to our hearts, the majority of us focus our attention on what our minds are telling us—which typically only reinforces the idea of our small, isolated, and separate self. We rely on this self, *its* direction, and all *its* interests and desires to find peace, happiness, and fulfillment. But as artist and teacher of Tibetan Buddhism Chagdud Tulku Rinpoche said, "If self-centeredness produced happiness, we would all be enlightened by now."[2] Goddamn, was he right.

I spent so many years of my life terrified (albeit unknowingly) of becoming intimate with my heart. I'm not talking about the watered-down, sentimental "heart" associated with things like Valentine's Day or romantic-comedy movies. No, I'm talking about the spiritual heart that is the absolute core of our being, the chakra or energy center that connects all our lower and higher energies, the place that houses our deepest wisdom.

During my early years of meditation, I was a mess, and not just the times when I was actively addicted, because at least then I felt I was in control of something (though of course that was the farthest thing from the truth). It was during my times of sobriety that I was the most scared. I didn't know a single thing about who I really was, and I'm not even talking about the deeper, esoteric "me," but the train wreck of a face I'd see staring back at me in the mirror every time I looked.

I was trying to better myself (whoever that self was), but was still skeptical about the effectiveness of meditation and had plenty of reservations about the whole "spirituality" thing. Through this fear and uncertainty, I kept my heart at bay. I was still under the impression that meditation was supposed to make me feel awesome and somehow make everything in my life better. While I sat on my cushion and painful thoughts and emotions arose, I mistakenly believed I was "failing at being spiritual" because that's not what I'd associated with meditation and spirituality. I had a naïve picture that being spiritual was about always feeling blissed-out and filled with light and love, so I would unskillfully use various breathing techniques and mantras (phrases or sounds repeated verbally or mentally) to suppress the negativity and hurt when they arose rather than acknowledging them and breathing in the pain, the fire of my experience.

Breathing techniques and mantras are wonderful tools, but *not* when they are a means of aversion. By using these practices to suppress my painful thoughts, emotions, and memories, I kept myself locked in a cycle of unnecessary pain and suffering for many years. In retrospect, I also came to see that the numerous relapses with drugs and alcohol I experienced during my struggles with sobriety were a direct result of this avoidance—an avoidance that perpetuated my unwillingness to face and deal with my life as it was falling apart around me.

Even after having learned this lesson the hard way, there are *still* times when I fall back into my old patterns (though thankfully not drugs and alcohol). For example, I recently relocated from Connecticut to Ottawa, Ontario, in Canada, where my wife, Jenn, is from. A few months before moving to Ottawa, I had the opportunity to spend a week there to get familiar with my new surroundings. I still had a bunch of engagements to fulfill in Connecticut before making the full-on move, but this was a great opportunity to check things out in the place I'd soon be calling home. I loved everything about it. There was no shortage of eclectic folks, things to do, and even a beautiful river with a running path along it directly across the street from our place. Plus, Jenn's family was really great and very welcoming, so I found myself comfortable, as if it were almost home—except, it wasn't, at least not yet.

While I was there, I thought about how excited I was to be finally moving in with my wife and stepdaughter. (We'd had a nightmare of a time with our sponsorship application that lasted fifteen months.) That's when it really hit me that I'd be leaving behind everything I knew: family, friends, local music venues, spiritual community—all of it. Everything in my life was about to change in the biggest way possible, and I began freaking out.

Over the course of that week, I watched myself eat super-unhealthy foods in the same exact way I used to drink and do drugs. No matter how much I'd already eaten, I went back for more: more cookies, more pizza, more candy, more whatever, in a futile attempt to mask the arising anxiety and fear within me. I was scared to be vulnerable and to touch my experience of fear, anxiety, and uncertainty directly, and this was how I handled it. I even took things a step further by running between seven and ten miles a day, not for health reasons, like normal, but to offset my feeling like shit because of how I was eating. What a cycle. I ended up running sixty-four miles that week and *still* managed to put on a few pounds. That's how out of control I was.

The whole ordeal—from the eating to running to consciously being aware of it all going down while keeping my heart completely closed to the situation—was fucking disgusting. As with anything in life, though, you live, you learn, and you move on (or you don't, and just keep yourself stuck in an ongoing cycle of shit).

As human beings, I believe we all share the desire to be free of pain and suffering. For many of us, as we progress on our spiritual paths, this desire matures from a personal wish and aspiration to one that is global, meaning that we wish for all beings to be free from pain and suffering. This maturation of our desire—from personal to global—is a result of our awakening heart-mind. *Bodhichitta* is a word frequently used in Buddhism to describe this state of awakened heart-mind. It is a Sanskrit word, with *bodhi* meaning "awake" or "enlightened," and *chitta* meaning "mind" or "heart."

And so bodhichitta—our awakened (or awakening) heart-mind—becomes our compassionate desire to realize our true Self (or nonself in Buddhist terms) for the benefit of all beings, a most noble desire and undertaking, for sure. In order for us to fully develop bodhichitta, we must get raw and intimate with ourselves first, laying our hearts' armor aside to look at and touch the place of pain and suffering that resides in our innermost selves.

Regarding bodhichitta, Pema Chödrön wrote in her book *The Places That Scare You:*

> Bodhichitta is also equated, in part, with compassion—our
> ability to feel the pain that we share with others. Without
> realizing it we continually shield ourselves from this pain
> because it scares us. We put up protective walls made
> of opinions, prejudices, and strategies, barriers that
> are built on a deep fear of being hurt. These walls are
> further fortified by emotions of all kinds: anger, craving,

indifference, jealousy and envy, arrogance, and pride. But fortunately for us, the soft spot—our innate ability to love and to care about things—is like a crack in these walls we erect. It's a natural opening in the barriers we create when we're afraid. With practice we can learn to find this opening. We can learn to seize that vulnerable moment—love, gratitude, loneliness, embarrassment, inadequacy—to awaken bodhichitta.[3]

The thought of getting raw with ourselves in this way can certainly be some scary shit and curb people's motivation for cultivating bodhichitta. The good news is that by facing our pain and touching our hearts directly, we begin breaking the monotonous cycle of pain. As we break this cycle, we make ourselves more available to the totality of life. The hurt will be there regardless of whether we chose to acknowledge and work with it or not, so why not just get on getting on with it?

Sometimes this work can get really heavy, and so the guidance of spiritual communities, psychotherapists, teachers, or any other supportive means that feels right for you is highly recommended. Hell, I'd recommend it even during the times that aren't so heavy. Remember, tune in to your heart, feel what's right for you, and roll with that.

Accepting ourselves fully in all of our perfect imperfections while taking an honest and fearless look at our naked selves, acknowledging both our frailty and the glory in the same glance, is not easy. It can be jarring to realize just how far we've actually gone to avoid feeling our feelings, which for many of us includes creating "protective walls made of opinions, prejudices, and strategies, barriers that are built on a deep fear of being hurt," as Pema said.

Poet Rainer Maria Rilke shared some encouragement that may help us through our difficult times when he wrote, "Let everything happen to you: beauty and terror. Just keep going. No feeling is final."[4] How I wish I'd remembered those words while I was binging-out in Ottawa. It's so important to remember that no feeling is final while we're working through life's shitstorms (big and small) because it's in this remembrance that we muster the courage to carry on—recognizing that our current experience of dis-ease is, in fact, only temporary.

As we intimately touch our pain and relate directly to life, we're no longer living in fear. Instead, we're reclaiming responsibility for our own well-being, not only for ourselves but also so that we can share it with others. We're developing the heart of a warrior, not in the traditional sense of warfare but rather in the way Chögyam Trungpa defined it, which was with qualities such as fearlessness and gentleness.

It's through our fearlessness and gentleness that we're able to see that Everything Mind not only includes spiritual platitudes (like the love-and-light I mistakenly believed was all there was to it back in my early days on the path), but pain and brokenness as well. In the following chapters, I'll explore ways to work with our pain, our brokenness, and the associated negative energies when we make ourselves available to the healing and compassionate force of bodhichitta.

Belief shaken to the core
Upon the sight of the other shore.

YOB, "UPON THE SIGHT OF THE OTHER SHORE"

5

FOR THE LOVE OF THE WOUNDED

Author and mystic Caroline Myss created a word that I love: *woundology.* It describes the way in which some people define themselves by their emotional, physical, and social wounds. It's so easy to suffer from woundology because when we face our pain, becoming intimate with the many ways in which it manifests (both internally and externally, from heartbreak to drug consumption, depression to excessive shopping), we can empower ourselves. Perhaps it's the first time in our lives when we're acknowledging and conquering a fear that's kept the deepest potential of our well-being—the experience of true joy, peace, and equanimity—just out of reach.

What happens to some of us as we experience ownership of our wounds is that we (consciously or unconsciously) create a new identity for ourselves. Besides the empowering quality of finally facing and owning our brokenness—the unresolved pieces buried deep within us after losing a loved one, a job, a friend, or resulting from any of life's numerous tragic situations—there is often also the sympathetic response and support we receive from those we share our difficult times with.

It's wonderful to receive empathy (rather than sympathy) and support from others during our healing process; I'm definitely not trying to say otherwise. I've experienced firsthand the power and difference they can make. I've been exceptionally fortunate to have the support of my family through my process of recovery from addiction. Unfortunately, many addicts can't say this because their families have written them off due to the addicts' using behavior and the pain inflicted on their families' lives. I don't know why I've been so blessed, but I can say that it's made a world of difference in my own personal recovery.

Take my brother, for example. He witnessed firsthand the complete and utter mess my life was for many years. He visited me in emergency rooms and rehabs, yet he never turned his back on me. He didn't enable me or support my behavior while I was actively using, but he never wrote me off, and I'm so grateful for that. This is the kind of person he is: While I was in my last treatment center, I asked him to help me sell my drums because I needed the money for the facility's co-payment. He said he'd help and go take some pictures of my drums to post online. But what he actually did after that was "buy" them himself, which meant he gave me the money for treatment, left the drums where they were, and allowed me to "buy" them back whenever I could afford to (which I did shortly after getting home). The importance and blessing of having people like him and my parents (who have also gone above and beyond in their support) in my life have never been lost on me, *ever.*

Sympathy and support, however, should never be at the expense of the actual healing itself, which, luckily in my case, it wasn't. This kind of care and attention can be extremely comforting, but, holy shit, that support can also be highly addictive. The problem creeps in when people sabotage their healing process because, usually unknowingly, they have learned to be comfortable in their discomfort so that they can maintain their wounded identity and continue to receive sympathy and support from others.

I've been guilty of woundology in the past: identifying myself as an addict and finding comfort in the sympathy it garnered me from others (though, I've received plenty of judgment as well). I *do* live with the disease of addiction. That is true. It would be irresponsible for me to lose sight of this fact and not do what I need to in order to maintain my recovery.

To base my entire identity, on the physical level, *exclusively* on being an addict (or even a recovering addict) is so limiting. I'm not ashamed or embarrassed to call myself a recovering addict because it's a part of my story. It has allowed me the wonderful opportunity of connecting with many people the world over on a deep level that I otherwise wouldn't have been able to, and for that I'm grateful. But being a recovering addict is only a *part* of who I am. Honoring that part of my life, without it defining me, has allowed me to break the chains of remaining actively wounded. It has also significantly helped to heal not all but a lot of the wreckage of my past, while still honoring that I have a real disease that *can kill me* if I'm not vigilant. For example, I fully recognize that I can't change my past actions. However, by making an effort to be the best possible person I can be today and being of service whenever and wherever possible in whatever capacity I'm able, I'm doing my part in trying to be of service to humanity, rather than just myself (which is all I used to be concerned about), and with that comes healing.

Now, I'm referencing addiction, pain, and created identities in relation to drugs and alcohol because that's my experience, but they apply to things like food, shopping, sex, spiritual practices (oh yes, they can be highly addicting too), TV, thinking, video games, and anything else that's out of our control. Addictions are serious issues that for some people require professional help, especially during the early stages of recovery.

Obviously, it's not only addicts who get wrapped up in the stories of their lives, creating identities around them. Everyone is subject to this. It's not always identities based on pain or tragedy either. Success stories are just as enticing to build a sense of self around: rich, famous, CEO, doctor, guru, lawyer, and so on. But think about this for a second: *What if* we made the conscious decision to let go of all the stories about who we think we are and instead allowed those stories to represent who we used to be? Shit, while we're at it, what if we let go of the stories altogether?

I'm not trying to make light of our life experiences, because they have and will continue to shape who we are as people. But what if we didn't rely on them to define us? The difficulties we face, when worked with skillfully, are an amazing opportunity for us to cultivate inner strength and emotional maturity. For many of us, the consequences of these difficulties sparked our interest in spirituality in the first place.

To help put this into greater perspective, think for a moment about all the identities you've already lived so far. When I was a child, I played soccer and hockey, and was a skateboarder in elementary school and proudly displayed my various attire—from sporty team jackets to Powell Peralta T-shirts and Vision Street Wear shorts—while walking the elementary-school hallways. I remember thinking to myself that I was extra cool because I identified as both an athlete and a rebel skateboarder. (Hey, this was back in the '80s when skateboarding was still an act of rebellion.)

As I moved on to middle and high school, I continued skateboarding, but left sports behind for music, learning to play bass, guitar, and drums. I replaced my team jackets with punk, hardcore, and hip-hop T-shirts (some things never change), and began identifying myself as a hardcore kid. And since high school, I've experienced and identified myself as a number of other things: vegan; born-again Christian; college dropout; shitty boyfriend to various girlfriends; vegetarian; mental patient diagnosed with bipolar disorder, depression, and suicidal ideation; indie rocker; omnivore; aspiring bodhisattva; welfare recipient; spiritual director; husband, stepfather, and son; author—all of which only begin to comprise who I am.

It's when I take an honest look at all this—my victories, failures, dreams, addictions, ideas, and memories—that I'm able to see the places where my greatest attachments (both negative and positive) are. These places, if not worked with skillfully, will lead to suffering. As we become lost in our identification with any particular thing, we set ourselves up for suffering. We cling to impermanent things, but anything that is impermanent (which is every single thing in our day-to-day physical reality) is an unreliable source of true and lasting peace. *True peace* is a formless quality that can't be found in the ever-changing and temporary world of form.

I'm not saying you shouldn't own your roles. In fact, quite the opposite: Own the shit out of them! Be an amazing parent, husband, wife, son, daughter, teacher, student, Buddhist, musician, Christian, skateboarder, yogi, or whatever else, but do so (as best you can) from a place of loving Witnessing Awareness instead of getting stuck in any particular role. This may sound like a form of detachment, which in a way it is, but it's not detachment in the sense of indifference. If anything, this form of detaching our identity from a "doer" frees our hearts and minds to be present in the moment with others. We still play our roles and do what we need to do, but now we're doing so from a place of compassion, awareness, and loving-kindness that benefits all beings.

Can you even begin to imagine the amazing *Being* that you are when stripped of labels, thoughts, words, and identities? Or what your experience in this world would be like free of these constraints, residing in the place of Everything Mind, if even for only a moment? Well, that's all it takes—just one moment—because the truth is, that's all we ever have.

Right here.
Right now.
You are that You are.
An unbounded and absolutely brilliant Being.
One whom no identity could ever confine.
Remember Yourself.
Take a deep, conscious breath and own the infinitely incredible Being that you truly are. That we truly are.
Breathe it in as if it were your last breath.
Because in this moment—
it is.
How absolutely perfect.

We're all going to die, all of us, what a circus!
That alone should make us love each other
but it doesn't. We are terrorized and flattened
by trivialities, we are eaten up by nothing.

CHARLES BUKOWSKI

LAST NIGHT OF THE EARTH

A friend recently asked me, "If you had to recommend the most spiritually inspiring and fulfilling book you've ever read, what would it be?"

"Christ," I replied, "how does one even begin to answer that?" I figured I'd give it a shot, though, so I started milling over some of my favorites like *Cutting Through Spiritual Materialism* by Chögyam Trungpa, *Talks with Ramana Maharshi* by Ramana Maharshi, *Be Here Now* by Ram Dass, *A Brief History of Everything* by Ken Wilber, and *The Tibetan Book of Living and Dying* by Sogyal Rinpoche. I realized pretty quickly that there was no end to this list, so I opted for the easy way out and conceded that I couldn't possibly name just one.

Later that evening, while lying in bed reading the final book Charles Bukowski wrote before he died, *The Last Night of the*

Earth Poems, I thought about my friend's question again and was surprised that none of Bukowski's works had come to mind while I was mulling over my possible answers. Bukowski is my favorite writer and has been for many years, and while some would probably disagree with me, I find much of his work to be extremely spiritual.

I'll never forget the first Bukowski book I read: *Post Office.* It was a funny, sad, and relentless story about a hard-drinking, racetrack-betting man who was stuck at a shitty job with the US Postal Service. I laughed, I cringed, I felt disgusted, I was inspired (not so much by the bleak story, but by the honesty with which it was written), and at the end of the roughly three hours it took me to devour it, what I remember feeling the most was alive. That's pretty much how my relationship with Bukowski's works has been ever since—one of being shaken alive by his raw, ragged, and darkly humorous writing.

As I lay in bed reading *The Last Night of the Earth Poems*—a book in which Bukowski is preoccupied with death because he knows it's close—I really took to heart the depth of what he'd made me feel throughout the years. I thought about all the mornings when, hungover, I'd thumb through the pages of his books and find some semblance of peace in the miserable experiences he wrote about, helping me feel a little bit less alone. I also thought about the sober times I'd read his work, feeling gratitude for no longer losing my life to hangovers or to dragging my ass to work or the liquor store or the bar—situations Bukowski so vividly writes about. I also thought about his pain, his struggles, his small victories, his self-loathing, and finally, his Zen—because yes, even Bukowski had a bit of Zen about him, which he displayed most prominently in poems like "Warm Light." (I'd planned on sharing excerpts from this and a few of his other poems in this chapter, but getting permission to do so from another publisher can be a very pricey thing, and my pockets just aren't that deep. So my suggestion is to buy yourself a copy of any and all of Bukowski's books, but particularly *The Last Night of the Earth Poems*.) However, Bukowski never claimed to be spiritual or religious. In fact, in his writing and interviews, he made it quite clear that he didn't buy into the traditional God concept. Take, for example, the following quote from an interview he did with *LIFE* magazine in 1988:

> For those who believe in God, most of the big
> questions are answered. But for those of us who can't
> readily accept the God formula, the big answers don't
> remain stone-written. We adjust to new conditions
> and discoveries. We are pliable. Love need not be a
> command nor faith a dictum. I am my own god. We
> are here to unlearn the teachings of the church, state,
> and our educational system. We are here to drink beer.
> We are here to kill war. We are here to laugh at the
> odds and live our lives so well that Death will tremble
> to take us.[1]

This quote embodies spirituality because it's Bukowski expressing *his truth* as *he* experienced it in the moment. Sure, it may not sound traditionally spiritual in nature, but he made it very clear that he was in touch with his insides—his Everything Mind—in a real and raw way. And that is a huge part of what spirituality is all about. Bukowski even managed to evoke another spiritual master, His Holiness the Fourteenth Dalai Lama, when he said, "Love need not be a command nor faith a dictum," which is reminiscent of His Holiness's statement, "Love and Compassion are the true religions to me. But to develop this, we do not need to believe in any religion."

And I can't forget to mention the punk-rock ethics (things like "Question everything" and "Do it yourself"—which are deeply spiritual to me) that Bukowski covered in that quote, when he said, "We are here to unlearn the teachings of the church, state, and our educational system," which I couldn't agree with more. For the most part, unlearning the majority of bullshit we've been fed by many churches and much of organized religion as a whole (not to say it's all bad, because it's certainly not), state, and the educational system is one of the greatest gifts we can give ourselves, as it affords us the opportunity to live unbiased by mainstream propaganda and control. We do not need to be a robotic part of their agenda, pledging allegiance to capitalism, consumerism, and greed, greed, greed . . . but I'm getting a bit off topic.

Bukowski gives of himself completely, with unfiltered vulnerability. How many of us can honestly say we're able to do that, to become completely honest with ourselves, even if only while writing in a journal, let alone while being interviewed by a national magazine? Sure, Bukowski had scumbag tendencies—he was a hard-drinking womanizer among other things. I'm not advocating that he's the poster boy for positive inspiration, but he was willing to acknowledge the shitty things he did. He owned that. For example, in his poem "oh, I was a ladies' man!" Bukowski blatantly calls out his earlier womanizing ways. (Another poem I'd planned to excerpt for you here, until I saw the cost. Did I mention you should buy *The Last Night of the Earth Poems* yet?)

Bukowski's unflinching honesty with himself has certainly inspired me to get honest in my own life and spiritual practice. I understand that taking a look at the unsavory parts of ourselves is never fun (and also doesn't need to be done in the self-loathing way Bukowski often chose), but I believe we could all take a page from Bukowski's books in becoming more honest and raw with ourselves, our motives, our intentions, and where we're really at in life.

Most of us are afraid to let some things inside of us out. Maybe we're afraid of what others will think, maybe we're afraid of failure, or hell, maybe we're even afraid of success. Whatever the case may be, Bukowski candidly shares with us his experience of keeping things locked inside. In this excerpt from his poem "the bluebird," (okay, I splurged a bit for you, dear reader) he writes:

> there's a bluebird in my heart that
> wants to get out
> but I'm too clever, I only let him out
> at night sometimes
> when everybody's asleep.
> I say, I know that you're there,
> so don't be
> sad.[2]

Well, there's a bluebird in my heart, *too.* One that I've kept hidden for much of my life. But thanks to the inspiration of Bukowski, complemented by other spiritual teachers and practices, today my bluebird is a little freer than it was yesterday. And that freedom continues to grow a bit with each passing day.

So, what *is* the most spiritually inspiring and fulfilling book I've ever read? Well, I still don't have an answer, but what I can say is that *The Last Night of the Earth Poems,* as well as much of Bukowski's other writing, is definitely up there. The fucking Zen of Bukowski . . . who'd have thought?

It's times like these
You learn to live again . . .

FOO FIGHTERS, "TIMES LIKE THESE"

7

BLOOD, BROKEN BONES, VIOLENCE, AND OTHER JOYS OF MEDITATION

We can't all be poets like Bukowski, but there is no shortage of other routes to cultivating Everything Mind. One of the most honest, direct, rugged, and raw (like Bukowski's style) methods is meditation. It's no secret that the benefits of meditation are well worth overcoming any resistance we may encounter to taking up a practice. Who wouldn't like to feel less stress, have lower blood pressure, increased calm, and greater focus in their daily lives, not to mention a more intimate connection with their Divine Self . . . and *for free?* Shit, you can't go wrong.

In his book *Hardcore Zen,* Brad Warner writes, "Your life is yours alone, and to miss your life is the most tragic thing that could happen. So sit down, shut up, and take a look at it."[1] Besides making an important point—that to miss out on our lives is one of the most tragic things that could happen—he essentially gives us the quick-and-dirty version of how to meditate, which could alternatively be said as "Sit down, shut up, and listen." When it comes to the practice of meditation itself, sure, there are suggestions for how to sit, place our hands, and breathe (all of which we'll cover later), but the essence of meditation really is that simple. Just sit down, shut up, and listen.

Now, I feel it's only fair to forewarn those new to meditation that the practice doesn't always consist of blissed-out states of white light and heavenly choruses. No, meditation can be extremely brutal. I don't mean brutal in the physical sense, like when our knees hurt from sitting for extended periods of time, but rather, brutal in the mental and emotional sense—that's where things can get exceptionally difficult and dark.

I recently experienced one of these brutal meditations, one that left me asking myself, "Is this really worth it?" As I sat, I watched a flurry of various painful memories arise from the wreckage of my past, seemingly out of nowhere. I saw my parents' faces looking in on me while I was strapped to a bed in an emergency room, out of my mind on drugs and alcohol. I saw myself chugging a pint of cheap vodka while on my way to pick up a friend to take her to get an abortion because I had woken up going through withdrawals and couldn't do it any other way. I saw myself crying, throwing up, punching walls, and cutting various body parts just so I could feel something. What hurt most of all as I relived these experiences was how deeply I felt the pain—both mine and others'—that came along with these memories.

Of course, once the intense feelings subsided, the answer to whether meditation was worth it or not was still undeniably yes. Yet, for many of us with complicated and even sordid histories, which include things like blood, broken bones, violence, DUIs, blackouts, and suicide attempts, our experiences on the cushion may at times be unpleasant enough to make us question why we're even practicing in the first place. Didn't we start meditating because we heard it would bring greater peace and joy into our lives? Well, it will . . . eventually; but for some of us, it just takes a bit longer.

I lived to drink alcohol and consume whatever other drugs were available, *and* I used these substances to live. This cycle of insanity dictated many years of my life. Although today I'm free from that insidious lifestyle, the painful memories remain. So why do people like me meditate? Why do we stay present with these experiences in meditation when we could just as easily escape through any number of life's limitless distractions? For me, it's because, no matter how uncomfortable meditation may get at times, deep down I know that my only other option is to revert to my old ways of living.

It's through learning to sit in meditation with a patient and open heart that I found the strength to face pain when it arises; to fearlessly stay with whatever life presents me in any given moment (on a good day); to walk through the difficult times rather than run away from them and numb myself with drugs, alcohol, food, sex, video games, movies, or whatever. Don't get me wrong—the temptation to take the easy way out still arises, and since nobody is perfect, there have been, and still are, times when I succumb in one way or another. These times can be beneficial as well. If we can muster the courage to consciously look at where things started to head south—before we began acting out or shooting up or using material objects as a means of avoidance—we can learn to see the root cause of *where* and *why* things began to fall apart. As we move forward, we can be more mindful of our self-defeating behavioral patterns and do our best to avoid falling back into them.

Still, some days can suck so incredibly much that the idea of just dropping out sounds great. These are the times when looking at our lives and ourselves from a place of compassion can become wonderful reminders of just how great today actually is. Why is today great? Well, we're alive and breathing, so there's a start. Seriously, if we're practicing any form of conscious living, that's huge! That's inspired living. As we learn to live more consciously, we learn to say yes to life, with the understanding that every single thing, both good and bad, is of equal value and importance on our path. Each encounter can be our teacher, our curriculum, or our guru when approached from a place of sincere curiosity, openness, and acceptance. This is Everything Mind.

The discomfort we feel at times in meditation isn't fun, but in comparison to the alternative—staying locked in a cycle of pain, dis-ease, and self-medication—is there any question that meditation isn't worth it? When we keep an open heart to the difficult times in life, we naturally cultivate an ever-growing amount of compassion for ourselves and others. Not to mention we'll be much better equipped to face the incredibly difficult shitstorms life inevitably sends our way from time to time.

Inspired living isn't always pretty. It isn't always fun. In fact, I've found that the most inspired times I've experienced since setting out on the spiritual path are when I consciously honor, face, and extend love and compassion to pain when it arises. Pain that is the result of the many fucked-up things I've done in my past. It's through facing and working with this pain, this wreckage of my past, that I heal and release it. With each broken piece I mend, I'm capable of sharing that much more love with all beings and myself.

Later on in the book, I'll share a very powerful practice about how to extend love and compassion to pain when it arises, but first things first: breath awareness.

Feelings come and go like clouds in a windy sky.
Conscious breathing is my anchor.

THICH NHAT HANH

PRACTICE

BREATH AWARENESS

It can't be all talking; there has to be some doing as well, so let's get started. Here's a little practice that's simple, easy, and will provide real-time results. It's based on *susokukan,* a kind of counting meditation which is the first training step in Zen meditation and is one of the most convenient practices I know for relieving stress, anxiety, fear, and worry, *and* for anchoring ourselves in the present moment of Everything Mind—the place where we touch the truest depths of our spiritual selves.

Simply stated, we're going to focus on our breath. Okay, there's a little more to it than just that, but not much. Begin by bringing your awareness to the breathing that's already naturally happening in your body, and then on your next in-breath (breathing through either your nose or your mouth, whichever is more comfortable for you), mentally note the number *one* to yourself. Then, on your out-breath, mentally note the number *two*. Continue this cycle of counting—one, two, three, four—until you arrive at ten on the out-breath; then begin again at one. (Some teachers ask their students to count the entire cycle of in- *and* out-breath as *one,* then to repeat that, counting as high as one hundred. Please feel free to use this method as well.)

You can do as many cycles of this focused breathing as you'd like, remembering that even just one conscious breath, let alone an entire cycle, is great for developing your concentration and presence in the moment. That's it. Oh . . . except for one minor detail. Any time you find your mind wandering while you're counting your breath, start over at *one.* (No cheating.) I guarantee you that this practice sounds easier than it is, so take your time with it and remember, it's not a competition.

Traditional Zen teachers recommend doing susokukan with open eyes and a lowered gaze, but I prefer to practice with my eyes closed whenever possible. That's not always an option, however, and the practice can work just as well with eyes open. At first, it's a bit trickier to stay focused with your eyes opened, but with a little time and practice, you'll find yourself attentively breathing in public places, with eyes open, and doing so with minimal effort.

Now, if you're feeling extra adventurous, here's another simple practice based on yogic breathing called *deergha swasam,* which you can add to your repertoire. It's a three-part breath practice (which is done all in one consecutive breath). The first part begins with breathing deeply into your belly until it fills with air. Once it's filled (while still continuing the same in-breath), breathe into your midsection (rib-cage area) until that's full, which is part two (and again, still on the same in-breath). On part three (and yes, still the same breath), fill your entire chest with air. That's the first half of the practice: breathing deeply into your belly, midsection, and chest until each section is full.

The second part of the practice is essentially the same thing, except you're exhaling. So on your out-breath, begin by breathing out the air from your chest until it's empty, and then your midsection until that's empty, and finally, exhale the air from your belly until that's empty.

Once you've finished the three parts of both the inhale and the exhale, that's one cycle. It may take a moment or two to get this practice down, but it's simple once you do it. (Start with five minutes at a time and increase from there.) I used to teach this three-part breath technique to elementary-school students. So if they could do it, I know you can too. If it helps, reread that last sentence while imagining R. Kelly's "I Believe I Can Fly" playing in the background because, yes, I believe you can fly . . . and touch the sky . . . and do this breathing practice. You're incredible, you magnificent creature, you.

Take the rose by the thorns.
Hope for sun, but here's the storm.

FUCKED UP, "THE OTHER SHOE"

LEFT BEHIND

Early in 2014, I met a lovely woman. She'd heard a bit about my story through a friend of my mother's and was particularly interested in the fact that I was in recovery from drug addiction since her son also struggled with it. While we spoke, she told me about how, in the hopes of finding some clarity, she had felt compelled to meet me because she wanted to hear directly from someone who'd lived through addiction. She was at a loss about how to help her son.

There were two reasons this was a particularly tough conversation for me. The first was that I could see my own mother in this poor woman. The second was because any time someone is caught in the grips of addiction, there's very little anyone else can do to get them to stop, which leaves loved ones in a rather hopeless situation. It's not exactly that loved ones can't do anything. Interventions can be helpful, though the success rate isn't the greatest. Breaking the codependent relationships that support the addicts' behavior can sometimes get them to seek treatment because they have nothing left. The truth of the matter, though, is that for *most* addicts (not all) it's not until they've had enough *themselves* and hit whatever bottoms they need to hit that they are compelled to stop. It's then that they have the best possible chance at recovery. Unfortunately, many addicts die before ever reaching the place of "enough."

As the kind woman and I continued our conversation, I found that the best thing I could do for her was to offer some words of hope. I shared my own experience and the hardships I had faced and endured. I was aware of a sadness arising in me while I spoke with her. In the back of my mind, I was thinking about how many people I'd seen die because of this fucking disease, and I hoped that her son wouldn't become one of them.

I also emphasized the importance of taking care of herself, something a lot of family members of active addicts overlook because they're so caught up in the pain their loved ones are enduring. Often without even recognizing it, family members will allow themselves to become extremely unhealthy on mental, emotional, physical, and spiritual levels—and this is completely understandable. The problem is that when they neglect to take care of themselves, their stress level and general lack of well-being carry over into their other relationships—family and friends, work, and life in general—which does no one any good. It can seem extremely selfish to want to take care of ourselves when someone we love so dearly is hurting in such a deep way, but there's no amount of sadness we can bring upon ourselves that will ever make them better, happier, or healthier. The choice to take care of ourselves consciously and compassionately, while not always an easy one, is one that's still important for us to make.

When the woman and I finished our conversation, I gave her a copy of my book to give to her son in the hopes that maybe it would inspire him to seek help. I made sure to let her know that my contact info was in the back and that I'd be happy to talk with him if he was ever interested.

Unfortunately, I never got that opportunity because a few weeks later he died from an overdose. My heart was extremely heavy with this news, as it always is when I hear about another life lost to addiction. I'll never get used to that kind of sorrow, and I don't want to. I can't even begin to imagine the pain the woman and her husband (who was the one who discovered their deceased son in their home) went through—the same pain I know my own mother, father, wife, stepdaughter, and family would experience if I were to become another statistic, losing my life unnecessarily to drugs.

My heart and prayers still go out to that woman and her husband, and the countless others who will grieve the loss of loved ones who died before their time because of addiction. But there is hope, whether it's through the 12-step fellowships, spiritual communities, yoga, refuge recovery, or any number of other methods people use to recover successfully. *There is hope* and *recovery is possible!* If you or a loved one are struggling with addiction and reading these words, please know that you are never, ever alone. We can, and *do,* recover from addiction. There's a quote that's often attributed to the Buddha, and although it's been refuted as a "fake Buddha quote," regardless of who said it, I feel it's really applicable here. So, as *someone* once said, "You, yourself, as much as anybody in the entire universe, deserve your love and affection."

It's said that addiction is cunning, baffling, and powerful, and even that doesn't begin to cover it. Addiction is a real disease that is responsible for the destruction of countless lives and unimaginable heartbreak. It does not discriminate. However, neither does recovery. So please, don't give up on yourselves or your loved ones who are struggling. Although there is no shortage of tragic stories, there's also no shortage of miracle stories. There is hope until our last breath. That is why, no matter what our addiction, no matter why we are suffering, it's important to take up a spiritual path, to abide in Everything Mind. Tomorrow may be too late.

PRACTICE

MEDICINE BUDDHA

The opportunities to practice are as myriad as the ways they can heal and give us tools when the going gets tough. I recently faced a situation in which it looked like Abby's (our roughly twelve-year-old basset hound) life was ending. She'd been sick off and on for a year with various stomach issues, but on this particular morning, she was sicker than we'd ever seen her. She was sprawled out on the kitchen floor in virtually the same exact place—and eerily in the same exact position—where just two years prior, our other dog, Onyx (a beautiful bloodhound/ Labrador mix), had passed away.

Abby's breathing was labored, and she could barely open her eyes. As I sat down on the floor with her, she tried to get up, only to fall, after which she gave up and went back to her shallow breathing. Sitting there alone with Abby that morning, I cried the hardest I'd cried since Onyx passed away. With tears streaming down my face, I began to thank her for being such an amazing dog and for all the wonderful memories she'd given me. As I continued mustering words to express how much she meant to me, I recognized that through the storm of emotions thrashing about within me, I was still there, present in the moment—present with all that was happening. My heart, while hurting terribly, was open to the entire experience, and my mind filled with an equanimity that I could only credit to years of meditation practice.

As I continued to cry, a memory came to mind from when I attended a Medicine Buddha ceremony given by the Venerable Khensur Rinpoche Lobsang Tenzin at Chenrezig Tibetan Buddhist Center in Middletown, Connecticut. Within the Mahayana Buddhist tradition, there are numerous Buddhas that represent different aspects of Buddha-nature, such as compassion, emptiness, and wisdom. The Medicine Buddha represents healing. It's believed that by invoking the Medicine Buddha's name or reciting the Medicine Buddha's mantra, we receive his spiritual, psychological, and physical healing.

Some say that even hearing the mantra recited just once can provide someone with a good rebirth or reincarnation. During the ceremony I attended, Rinpoche, who is from Tibet and received the Medicine Buddha transmission directly from His Holiness the Fourteenth Dalai Lama, taught us the Medicine Buddha mantra:

Tayata Om Bhekandze Bhekandze Maha Bhekanzde Randza Samungate Soha.

It was in remembering that promise of a good rebirth that I began reciting the words aloud for Abby:

Tayata Om Bhekandze Bhekandze Maha Bhekanzde
Randza Samungate Soha, Tayata Om Bhekandze

Bhekandze Maha Bhekanzde Randza Samungate Soha.
Tayata Om Bhekandze Bhekandze Maha Bhekanzde
Randza Samungate Soha, Tayata Om Bhekandze
Bhekandze Maha Bhekanzde Randza Samungate Soha.

I said the words repeatedly, tears still falling down my cheeks, with increasing peace and acceptance arising around the situation. My mother came home from work early, and we wrapped Abby in a blanket and took her to the vet's office. When we arrived, I carried Abby, believing those would be my final moments with her. A technician brought us into a room, and I set Abby down on the floor while we waited for the vet. After about five minutes, for no apparent reason, Abby stood up! She then began to walk around and even wag her tail.

She was still weak in her back legs and hobbled a bit, but she was up and moving. As completely overjoyed as I was, I still found what was happening extremely weird, like *The-Twilight-Zone* weird. My mother and I looked at one another and didn't know what to make of it. I was scared to get my hopes up because none of this made any sense. The vet came in a few minutes later, and she was stumped too. She took Abby to get X-rays, which showed that everything was fine internally. She also drew blood to have it tested, and the results came back normal.

As I write about this strange event, it's a few months after the fact, and Abby is completely back to normal—well, as normal as can be for an old girl like her. I don't want anyone to get the wrong impression and think that I attribute her miraculous recovery to my reciting the Medicine Buddha mantra (though, hey, you never know). The point I wish to emphasize is that through the repetitive use of the Medicine Buddha mantra, while in the face of what seemed like dire circumstances with Abby, a sense of peace, calm, and spacious acceptance arose around the heartbreak I was experiencing. In retrospect, I know it wasn't a coincidence that the Medicine Buddha mantra popped into my head in that moment, and the mantra is one that I've since brought back into a more regular rotation in my practice: for myself, for Abby, and for all beings.

(Note: About six months later, Abby became sick again. She was unable to walk or eat, so we took her back to the vet, and they found she had a stomach tumor. At her age, we were left only with the option of putting her to sleep so that she wouldn't suffer. As I write this updated note, it's two months after the fact, and it still pains me, as if it had just happened yesterday. I hold the Medicine Buddha mantra close to my heart, however, reciting it in gratitude for the twelve years I shared with Abby and for the gift of the extra six months we had together.)

> You're doomed! You're all doomed!

CRAZY RALPH, IN *FRIDAY THE 13TH*

9

DEATH IN THE AIR

As young boys, my friends and I—the sneaky little bastards that we were—would watch films like *A Nightmare on Elm Street* and *Friday the 13th* during sleepovers (unbeknownst to our parents, of course). Since that time, autumn, Halloween, and the celebration of all things spooky and unknown have held a special place in my heart. Any time you bring together monsters, zombies, and aliens with a shit ton of candy, well, what's not to love?

I recently found myself contemplating the cultural celebration known as Halloween while I stood in an extremely long line with my wife, waiting to embark on a forty-five-minute walk through a haunted-graveyard attraction in Connecticut. I became utterly fascinated with the fact that the month of October brings people together in celebration of things they would otherwise normally consider gross, barbaric, and evil.

I'm a complete weirdo and find all these things entertaining year-round. (Don't forget Everything Mind. It's *all* part of the path—dark and light.) As I stood there watching the "normal" (well for the most part anyway) people anticipating their turn in the graveyard, I found the celebration of blood, severed body parts, chainsaw-wielding maniacs, and death so fucking weird—the only reason they seemed to be there was because it was October.

Psychosocially speaking, there's a personality type called type T, which—if that's your type—means you're a stimulation-seeking, excitement-seeking, thrill-seeking, arousal-seeking, and risk-taking individual. (Think Keanu Reeves and Patrick Swayze in the film *Point Break*. That's right, "Vaya con Dios, brah.") So okay, maybe the thrill seekers waiting in line around me weren't as radical or extreme as Bodhi (Swayze) and Johnny Utah (Reeves), but this would explain some of their attraction to all things horror in October. However, not being type T myself, I was still at a loss.

With the exception of my near-death relationship with addiction, I'm typically the farthest thing from a thrill seeker. I've never been one to go on roller coasters. (Well, that's not entirely true. I did go on the Batman ride at Six Flags many years ago when I was shitfaced. Even then, I remember holding on for dear life, screaming like a child, with my eyes closed the entire time.) I've also never had any interest in other thrill-seeking behaviors such as bungee jumping or skydiving. Hell, if I'm in the front passenger seat of a car, and the person driving gets too close to the car in front of us, I'll push my foot down on the floor as if I had the ability to control the brakes myself. Yes, really.

While I continued standing there in line at the graveyard, thinking about all this, I remembered a concept from the great psychiatrist Carl Jung, one that he called the *shadow self.* The shadow self is an unconscious aspect of one's personality that the conscious ego doesn't identify. This resonates much more deeply with me than type T personality because the shadow self represents the denied aspects of who we are and the social masks we wear. When we deny certain unsavory parts of ourselves, we project them onto others and thus use them as scapegoats instead of facing our own unpleasant characteristics. So let's see here: Denied aspects of myself? *Check.* Projected them onto others? *Check.* Wore social masks? *Check.* Yes, these are all things I've been guilty of throughout the years and am still periodically guilty of today.

The idea of our shadow self always makes me think of Michael Myers in the *Halloween* movies and how he lurked in the shadows and stalked his victims before killing them. You kind of sense he's there, but because you don't actually see him, you just brush it off. This is similar to what most of us do with our shadow selves. (Bonus points for Michael, as I also find him eerily reminiscent of humanity's dark collective unconscious, all personified in one unrelenting, unremorseful, and evil-as-fuck being.)

In his book *The Integral Vision,* Ken Wilber offers a more applicable version of the shadow self and explains why it's not only important, but *necessary* for us as humans to work with and uncover our hidden shadows. Wilber writes:

> The "shadow" is a term representing the personal unconscious, or the psychological material that we repress, deny, dissociate, or disown. Unfortunately, denying this material doesn't make it go away; on the contrary, it returns to plague us with painful neurotic

symptoms, obsessions, fears, and anxieties. Uncovering, befriending, and re-owning this material is necessary not only for removing the painful symptoms, but for forming an accurate and healthy self-image.[1]

Another way to sum up our shadow self is this: any time we feel a strong emotional response to something outside of ourselves—another person, for example, or, even in my case, horror movies—that's the first sign our shadow self is acting up. For most of us, our experience of these emotions is typically followed by criticism and blame toward those outer elements in order to divert our attention away from the dirty little parts of ourselves we'd rather not acknowledge. When it comes to horror movies, I think my love for them (rather than criticism or blame) is partly because there's a guilt-free association with projecting some of the denied aspects of myself onto them. I'm not saying I have a hidden or denied taste for blood or murder, but there *is* a lot of pain and fear in horror movies, and there is definitely pain and fear within me as well.

The shadow self acts as a "shadow" for a reason; we're afraid of what we'll find out about ourselves when we shine a light on it and look. The good news, though, is that as we work on overcoming our fear about these hidden places inside of ourselves and take a closer look at these denied aspects of our shadow self, we liberate a lot of pent-up energy—energy that previously had been reserved for keeping those unsavory parts of ourselves hidden.

When we bring awareness to our emotional states and the corresponding ways in which we act toward others as a result, we take back control of our internal well-being—well, either that, or, we can keep going on autopilot and, as Pinhead from the *Hellraiser* movies so eloquently said, "Your suffering will be legendary, even in hell!" Whichever you'd prefer.

There comes a time in every man's life
When he's gotta handle shit up on his own.

THE PHARCYDE, "RUNNIN'"

PRACTICE

SHADOW SELF

There are a number of shadow work practices and great teachers on the subject, so if it's something that interests you (I truly can't stress the importance of this stuff enough), I'd recommend checking out writings by Carl Jung, Robert Augustus Masters, Ken Wilber, and others who go into significant depth. In the meantime, here's a quick practice to help get you started on uncovering, befriending, and re-owning your shadow.

- The best time to do this practice is either in the morning after you wake up, using someone who showed up in your dreams (if you're able to remember them), or in the evening before you go to bed, using someone from your day who elicited any kind of emotional response from you.

- When you have that person in mind, mentally face and talk to them. Discuss whatever came up for you in the dream or in person during the day (your thoughts, feelings, and emotions). Let it all out—you're doing this only mentally, so there's no reason to hold back.

- Next, become that other person and adopt their perspective. Face and speak to yourself as if you were them. As best as you can imagine, offer yourself their perspective of the experience and situation. This helps to take you out of yourself and to see what role you possibly played in whatever the situation was.

When I first learned this practice, I didn't really think anything would come from it. I didn't see how imaginary conversations and talking to myself could do a damn thing to unlock my Everything Mind. Through the years, however, I've found that this practice has really helped me understand and experience the ways I project my unconscious shadow emotions onto others.

Take sadness as an example. I used to seek out sadness in others so that instead of having to face and feel my own sadness, I could focus on, and feel, *theirs*. Through this behavior, I disowned my own sadness and projected it onto others. I was using their sadness as an excuse to feel sad rather than acknowledging and exploring the roots of my own. The difference may seem subtle, but any time we disassociate from parts of ourselves, no matter how small, it's never a healthy decision.

When we do shadow work, we're really digging into the core of our unconscious ugliness. We're uprooting the painful thoughts and memories we've consciously or unconsciously hidden away throughout our lives. Please know that shadow work can be heavy at times, and while it's great to start working with it on your own, for going deeper, it may be worth looking into going to a trained psychotherapist.

I mentioned earlier that I've periodically struggled with my eating habits, and in turn my weight. A few years ago, while doing shadow work, I stumbled upon at least one of the contributing factors. It was morning, and the previous night, I'd had a dream in which I ate constantly. I woke up feeling disgusted with myself and began the aforementioned shadow work practice.

As I thought about how disgusted I was with my behavior in the dream, and occasionally in real life as well, I saw the other me begin to get very sad. This was followed by "me" turning into a Little League baseball coach I had when I was a kid. . . . And then it hit me. I remembered the day we got our team uniforms and all put them on. Mine was particularly snug, and the coach said to me, in front of the rest of my team, "Looking good, Crisco." Everyone, including the coach and his assistants, proceeded to laugh. I don't think his comment was meant in a completely malicious way; however, it hurt me deeply enough that I had suppressed it since I was a kid.

After the initial residual pain from this deeply buried memory wore off, I began to feel a tremendous sense of peace and spaciousness arise within me. That's what happens when we do shadow work: we uncover and release these shit-tastic memories that have been buried for Christ-knows-how-long. With that, we also release the accompanying negative energy associated with them.

As with any practice, we do the best we can on any given day and trust in the process, understanding that shadow work can be a particularly difficult undertaking. In the spirit of complete honesty, shadow work for most of us is pretty much a forever thing—for where there is light, there is also a shadow. But in our shadow practice, we begin to integrate both. Ken Wilber really summed it up nicely when he wrote, "The shadow is just one tricky little son of a bitch, which I suppose is how you get to be the shadow in the first place."[1]

> I set this fire in my heart to
> compensate for this lost love.
>
> THREADBARE, "MIDAS"

10

ONE FOOT OUT OF HELL

ne thing that working with my shadow self—as well as the other practices covered throughout this book—has really helped me develop is compassion for all kinds of people. Being heavily tattooed with big holes in my earlobes, a skateboarder, and a fan of punk and hardcore music since my teenage years has left me all too familiar with judgmental people, especially since I grew up in a small town before these things started to become even somewhat socially acceptable.

Disapproving looks and comments under the breath—or in some cases to my face—have been commonplace throughout my life and have led me time and again to contemplate why people feel the need (or think they have the right) to pass judgment and write someone off based solely on outer appearances and lifestyle choices.

There's no simple answer. Each person is an individual with a unique set of circumstances that has led them to become who they are. One thing I've come to recognize about myself and my own judgments (because yes, I too am human and have no shortage of them) is that they're usually rooted in fear.

Over the last several years, I've watched how being a counterculturist, or *raging against the machine* (though truth be told, when I was younger, I often wasn't quite sure exactly what machine I was raging against), has often left *me* judgmental toward people who are celebrated by the mainstream media: from spiritual teachers to musicians, actors, and more. Don't get me wrong; I'm grateful for my punk/hardcore roots since they helped me dismantle a lot of the naiveté in my otherwise culturally conditioned mind, but I am definitely experiencing some of the residual effects in my adult life.

I've come to recognize a sincere fear within myself of appearing to be a "conformist" for nothing more than liking a popular band, reading one of Oprah's official book selections, or maybe, just maybe, even admitting that someone like Justin Timberlake actually has some legitimate talent. It's a fear of judgment from my underground, countercultural peers, but at the end of the day, isn't a close-minded judgment a close-minded judgment? Yup, I still have plenty of work cut out for myself too.

On a deeper level, there's the hateful rhetoric of racism, sexism, homophobia, and more. Let me be clear that I don't condone any sort of hate-fueled ideology, because close-minded ignorance definitely turns my stomach. Every time I see the news cover the Westboro Baptist Church protestors and their "God Hates Fags" signs or a KKK rally, I feel my entire body begin to tense up. Nevertheless, I'd be lying if I said it didn't also make me feel a deep sense of sadness and compassion for those people because I know their hate is rooted in fear. I spent the better part of my own life living from a place of fear too, though I'm thankful it never manifested in any of the aforementioned hate-spewing ways.

Living for many years as a hardcore addict, there were countless nights I would lie in a dark room, filled with fear, self-hatred, and a disdain for God (or whatever "it" was out there that created this whole insane goddamn world), wishing for death to take me. I lost so many years of my life to those experiences that now, having come out the other side of them, I can't help but have compassion for those who suffer. That includes *all forms of suffering* and *all who suffer,* even those who are filled with hate and prejudice. To me, it's obvious that they're the ones who are the most frightened. (Just a reminder: Everything Mind includes *everything.*)

Sometimes I'll take a minute and put myself in their shoes, imagining what it must be like to go to bed each night filled with so much anger, hatred, and fear. I'm sure that for the majority of them these feelings occur on an unconscious level. But no matter where they are, they are there. Whether those people realize it or not, it's making their lives what I could only imagine to be a complete living hell. Remember the shadow self and projection? Yeah, that.

When I sincerely try to envision the scared inner child housed within each one of those people, honestly, it becomes virtually impossible for me to muster any judgments to throw back on them, no matter how much I disagree with their beliefs and viewpoints. As crazy as this may sound, all I'm left with is the desire to hug each one of them. Instead of meeting their fear and hatred with fear and hatred of my own, I'd much rather look them in the eyes with compassionate understanding and tell them that it's going to be okay—that we've all suffered.

You might believe I'm naïve for thinking like this, and who knows, maybe I am, but it's what's in my heart. And if there's one thing I've learned in life, it's that when I quiet my mind and allow my heart to guide me, I've never been steered wrong.

Count your blessin's and mind yo business.

ATMOSPHERE, "LIKE THE REST OF US"

11

OUTSIDE THE CONFINES

It's not only racists, sexists, and homophobes who have closed minds. I find it very interesting to watch just how much some "spiritual" people get bent out of shape over other people who don't fit their image of what spirituality is supposed to look like. As I've mentioned, I have lots of tattoos. I honestly don't care if you're tattooed or not; I just happen to like them, and so I get them. As a result of said tattoos, however, more times than I care to remember, I've heard comments like, "Anyone who desecrates their bodies couldn't know the first thing about spirituality, compassion, loving-kindness, or well-being." I'm not singling anyone out here, because I've caught it from Christians, Buddhists, yogis, nondenominational spiritualists, and more.

It's not just those of us who are tattooed who are on the receiving end of this. The stereotypes often carry over to include people whose lifestyle and appearance deviate from what's traditionally considered "acceptable" as either a spiritual or cultural norm. This can include dyed hair, piercings, nontraditional attire, and a plethora of other material things that "don't fit the mold." It pretty much goes without saying that if you live life in a way that's different, you're subject to finding yourself on the receiving end of the occasional mockery by those who fear the unfamiliar, which is never a good time.

The thing is, no matter how closed off certain people are from a lifestyle they don't understand, it's not going to stop us. As with every generation, but perhaps most like the 1960s, younger people immersed in counterculture are speaking out. Like those who came before us, our hearts are dedicated to the revolution, to changing humanity for the better.

The number of young, independently minded spiritualists is growing, and for many, our conscious awareness and interests are shifting from that of ethnocentric (some of us) to worldcentric (all of us). What this means is that we're no longer interested only in the well-being of *our* friends, families, communities, nations, or even just ourselves. Rather, our focus has shifted toward the well-being of the entire global community. Sure, some of us may look funny to others, but isn't life's diversity something to be celebrated rather than scoffed at, especially when the "funny"-looking people are working toward making this world a better place?

I'm grateful to no longer feel the need to judge others whose outsides don't match mine, though it certainly wasn't always like that for me. Relinquishing superficial judgments is something I've worked on diligently. Through years of practice, today I can honestly say that I've made sincere progress. I don't give a shit about your style of dress, or haircut, or whatever other external things seemingly make us different. I'm much more interested in what's happening on the inside—what does your heart have to say?

When my first book, *Indie Spiritualist,* was published, I received criticism from some "spiritual" people, based solely on my outer appearance. What surprised me was that some of it came when two spiritual teachers I deeply respect, Ram Dass and Tara Brach, in support of the book's release, were kind enough to share the endorsements they'd written for it on their Facebook pages.

Both Ram Dass's and Tara's work have been extremely important in my life, so I was touched that they took the time to spread the word about mine. Their Facebook posts included a picture of me, clearly showing my heavily tattooed arms. In all fairness, the majority of the comments from people were very nice and supportive, but there were still those who felt the need to leave shitty remarks based on nothing more than my appearance. An example from Tara's page is, "I'm at a loss on how true wisdom can exist simultaneously with the obsession to tattoo your body. It would seem that seeing through the *maya* of social conditioning would include seeing the silliness of tattoos, especially many, many, many tattoos."

I posted this person's comment on my own Facebook page, as I was sincerely curious to hear what others thought. I'm completely aware that the responses shared with me may be biased since they came from people with similar ideas and values as mine, but here are a few of them:

My tattoo artist up in PA had a great bumper sticker in his studio. It said, "Your body is a temple. I'm just here to decorate the walls." I loved that sentiment while getting my back tattooed years ago, and I still love it today.

Love and tolerance is our code—but not necessarily everyone's!

It would seem that seeing through the maya of social conditioning would include seeing the silliness of judging someone by their surface appearance.

Have you ever seen the movie *Legends of the Fall?* There is a scene where Anthony Hopkins yells, "Fuck 'em!"

The *Legends of the Fall* comment was my personal favorite. Anyway, it's in the spirit of love and acceptance (a pretty universal spiritual theme) that I ask the people who still find it necessary to judge and vocalize their disapproval of those who are externally different: Why not try using difference as an opportunity to turn inward and explore why you are judgmental in the first place?

If you truly consider yourself spiritual, please take a moment to contemplate whether those who live differently from you or practice differently from you are affecting your life's well-being—spiritual or otherwise. If they're not, then why not continue to explore why you care? I'm offering you these questions from a sincere place, a place where we can attempt to find some reconciliation rather than create more separation.

Accepting one another for exactly who we are as we step foot onto the spiritual path is of paramount importance because—regardless of the differences in our personal tastes, styles, or beliefs—bettering ourselves through conscious, intentional living is always for the greater collective good, which includes *all of us.* Each moment any of us (and I mean *any* of us) sits in meditation, says a prayer, practices yoga, counts a mala or rosary bead, or takes a mindful breath while skateboarding, hiking, making love, or rocking out at a concert, we truly benefit all beings.

If your Everything Mind doesn't help you practice kindness, compassion, and acceptance, and include *everyone,* then what's the point?

Care about other people's approval
and you will always be their prisoner.

LAO TZU

THE CHEMISTRY OF COMMON LIFE

You know the old saying "Opinions are like assholes; everyone's got one"? Well, I think as was made clear in the last chapter, that's about as accurate a truth as any. However, unlike our actual need for an asshole (hey, man, it's the truth!), the majority of our opinions are not only unnecessary, but they're also a great source of suffering. I'm not saying opinions are necessarily bad. They're a natural part of the human experience, and we all have them (God knows I do). The suffering creeps in when people hold on to their opinions so tightly that they believe their ideas and views are the *complete* truth.

Unfortunately, when people come from this place of believing they have the ultimate truth, they shut themselves off from much of life. They're locked in a form of *nonvacancy,* which is to say, they're stuck in a place with no room for anything new to come in.

They're unable to hear or see anything outside of their own filtered projections; and with that, they miss the plain truth that in life, everything simply is as it is. (That is, until we begin judging situations and subsequently "create" the world we see.)

There are always at least three perspectives from which we can consider any experience: ours, theirs, and the experience itself without any opinions or judgments. Many people are unaware of this because they're complacent in their own way of seeing and aren't really interested in reevaluating their outdated paradigms. Lest we forget, familiarity breeds comfort. So let's say you're in your local bookstore, and you see a copy of *Everything Mind* sitting on the shelf. Most likely, since you recognize the book sitting there, you'll have some sort of reaction upon seeing it, thinking something like, "Cool, I dig that book." On the other hand, maybe someone else who read it really disliked it, and when they see it sitting on the same shelf, they think to themselves, "What a piece of shit."

Now of course, I hope your experience with this book is good rather than bad, but the thing is, the only truth about this book is that *it's just a book.* That's it. Sure, there are some thoughts, teachings, and experiences in it, and God knows I poured my entire heart, guts, and soul into it, but at the end of the day, it's just a book. We bring our own life experience into it, or to any other thing or occurrence in life, and this experience determines what is going to resonate with us or not. From there, our opinions about the book (or whatever) are created—good or bad.

If the book example didn't do it for you, here are a few more off the top of my head: the Montreal Canadians hockey team, Powell Peralta skateboards, *The Legend of Zelda* video game, Martin guitars, Johnny Cash, De La Soul, *Star Wars,* Jesus, Mike Patton, Shakti, Buddha, Chuck Palahniuk, Krishna, dogs, cats . . . get the point?

Some of these examples may have resonated as things you like, while others didn't. No matter what we think about them, remember that our thoughts—good, bad, or impartial—are always a direct result of our own perceptions, which have been conditioned by our life circumstances leading up to this point. This is not to say anyone's perceptions are better or worse than others, but that they are ours, and others' perceptions and experiences are theirs. Still, underneath it all, everything simply is as it is.

My humble suggestion would be that you try to remember this the next time you find yourself judging someone else for their likes, dislikes, or general viewpoints, because just like you, they are projecting their filtered perceptions onto the object or situation. Can you imagine how much more peace and cohesion there would be throughout the world if people made the conscious effort to really do this? I truly believe this isn't just some far-fetched dream, but something we can all do. But we have to actually *make the effort* to do it.

There have been times where things I've written didn't get the nicest feedback (as I mentioned before, there are some seriously grumpy "spiritual" people out there), and yeah, it bummed me out. But that was only until I reminded myself that their words and opinions were filtered through their experiences of what they read, having little to do with me at all. (I know I keep reiterating the filtered-projections point, but I'm really trying to plant some seeds here.)

On the other hand, the nice and complimentary remarks people have made about stuff I've written were also filtered through their experiences and have nothing to do with me either. Sure, I may have written the words, and of course I'm always touched and grateful for kind feedback—especially when something I wrote helped someone through a difficult time in their life—but good or bad, I remind myself that the feedback is always a result of (you guessed it) life experience and filters.

In 1997, a Toltec spiritualist from the Eagle Knight lineage named don Miguel Ruiz wrote a book called *The Four Agreements*. Not only did it change countless lives, but it also went on to become a *New York Times* bestseller for more than seven years and is the thirty-sixth bestselling book of the decade. (Hey, gotta give credit where credit's due, right?) The four agreements are:

1. Be impeccable with your word.
2. Don't take anything personally.
3. Don't make assumptions.
4. Always do your best.

They're all valuable, but it's don Miguel's second agreement, "Don't take anything personally," that illustrates precisely what I've been discussing in this chapter. About it he writes:

> Nothing other people do is because of you. It is because of themselves. All people live in their own dream, in their own mind; they are in a completely different world from the one we live in. When we take something personally, we make the assumption that they know what is in our world, and we try to impose our world on their world.
>
> Even when a situation seems so personal, even if others insult you directly, it has nothing to do with you. What they say, what they do, and the opinions they give are according to the agreements they have in their own minds. Their point of view comes from all the programming they received during domestication.[1]

We all have our own belief systems, created by our experiences, and it's through them that our attitudes, opinions, and lifestyles are formed. By recognizing this, we come to realize that taking things personally is a waste of time and energy, an insult to our own well-being.

Everything other people say and do is just a reflection of their internal world and beliefs, as is everything we say and do. And when we really take this to heart, we can allow others to be who they are, feel what they feel, think what they think, and say what they say, and not take any of it personally—good or bad. Because again, *it has nothing to do with us!*

As we begin to embrace this, life becomes friendlier. It's no longer an experience of "us against them." Nor do we cling to our thoughts and opinions as being definitively true, believing that others who don't see things our way are wrong. From this place of openness, we're able to realize that *we're both right.* In everyday life, we each experience our own truth. So why not just relax and learn to honor this among one another? (My one exception to this rule would most definitely be if someone's "truth" was inflicting harm. Then, it's not cool just to let it be, and skillfully addressing the situation would definitely be best.)

I'd like to note that I still catch myself in contradictions sometimes. Here I am writing about Everything Mind, our interconnectedness, and how spiritual life can be so awesome and sometimes beautiful—and it is—but just like anyone else, I have got some deeply rooted shit that needs to get weeded out. Just the other day, I was shopping in a packed grocery store, feeling extremely tired and hungry—basically in an overall bad mood—when I caught myself becoming extremely agitated by anyone in the store who cut me off, accidentally bumped into me, or even looked at me the wrong way, which basically consisted of everyone.

Even though I became aware of this happening, because I was in such a shitty mood I felt helpless to do anything about it—although of course I wasn't, not really. Once I left, I proceeded to mentally shit on myself for acting like such a prick. When I got home, I worked it out by practicing Tonglen (which we'll explore in the following practice), but still, what a shitty and unnecessary experience.

Thankfully, this sort of ridiculousness doesn't happen very often. But sometimes? Well, shit happens. Life is tough, and so much of it is a contradiction to begin with that it's not always easy to make sense of things. Just look at all the incredible beauty that surrounds us: nature, random acts of kindness, a child's laughter. All of which is happening simultaneously with the horrors of life: war, rape, and random acts of violence. This dichotomy can be overwhelming, but each of us can begin making a difference by cultivating the practice of not taking things so personally. I'm sure that sounds like a rather small offering in comparison to the pain and suffering that's happening throughout the world, and it is. But at least it's something, and it's doable, starting *right now.* By making even just this simple effort, we're cultivating greater peace and compassion for ourselves, for others, and for the world as a whole; and that's a start.

Compassion asks us to go where it hurts, to enter into the places of pain, to share in brokenness, fear, confusion, and anguish. Compassion challenges us to cry out with those in misery, to mourn with those who are lonely, to weep with those in tears. Compassion requires us to be weak with the weak, vulnerable with the vulnerable, and powerless with the powerless. Compassion means full immersion in the condition of being human.

HENRI J. M. NOUWEN

PRACTICE

TONGLEN

When I find myself becoming agitated with someone, I try to practice Tonglen (key word being "try"). Tonglen, a Tibetan word that American Buddhist Lama Surya Das describes as meaning "sending and receiving," is a breathing and visualization practice that helps us cultivate compassion and loving-kindness for all beings. It gives us the opportunity to connect deeply with both our own suffering and the suffering of the world. Sounds like fun, right? It's not all about doom and gloom, so don't worry.

The further we go into the practice of Tonglen, the more in tune our hearts become with their own natural compassion for all beings. We see more clearly that everyone truly is fighting their own battles in life. More often than not, these battles occur on an unconscious level, which is a huge part of the reason people often behave so miserably toward one another. I'm not here to make excuses for anyone, because we're all responsible for our own shit, but as we become more intimate with the suffering that is present within all life—including humans, animals, the earth—our hearts naturally begin to come from a place of compassion rather than aggression and defensiveness.

We often have the tendency to get lost in our pain—mental, emotional, and physical. We believe that *no one* could ever possibly understand what we're going through because *it's our pain, exclusive to us* as we experience it. With the concentrated practice of Tonglen, the intimate nature of the hurt we experience either directly or indirectly, through empathy for another, becomes less personal. We begin to see the hurt as a byproduct of the shared human experience, one that most definitely sucks at times but that need not define who we are, nor completely dictate our well-being.

- Begin the practice by sitting in whatever meditation posture is most comfortable. Next, while focusing on your breath, imagine that you're breathing in and out of your heart rather than your mouth or nostrils.

- Bring a sense of stillness and openness to the general experience of pain throughout the world. Our typical reaction to suffering is to try to push it away, to distract ourselves from it any way we can. With Tonglen, we learn to stop struggling against it. We relax our mind and open our heart, and as we do so, we cultivate a sense of trust in the process.

- Once you've anchored yourself in this cycle, begin the visualized exchange portion of Tonglen: continue breathing in the world's pain and suffering, and breath out an offering of peace, comfort, and relief to all beings that are experiencing pain.

- Now, on your in-breath, breathe in a textured visualization of thick, heavy, and hot black smoke (or any other image that coincides for you with pain and suffering). Then, on the out-breath, send out qualities that are light and cool, visualizing something like moonlight, a gentle stream, or a soft cloud (or again, whatever imagery represents light and cool for you). Continue breathing in this way for a few minutes, and really embody the experience.

- When we do this, we're flipping the script on the aversion we usually have toward suffering, bringing acceptance to what we'd normally not want any part of—not just our pain and suffering but the entire world's collective pain and dis-ease as well. Breathing out, we send an aspiration of love, compassion, and fearlessness to the world. We're offering everyone, everywhere, every ounce of our own well-being with the aspiration that they may enjoy freedom from suffering. (A quick note: Do your best to keep the in-breath and the out-breath evenly balanced. For example, don't make the in-breaths shorter because they are unpleasant, or allow the out-breaths to be longer because they feel good.)

That's the traditional practice of Tonglen. Another way in which we can use it is by practicing for someone or something specific. For example, if we're practicing for our heartbroken friend who just lost their dog, we breathe in the pain of all beings who are experiencing heartbreak from the loss of a pet. Then we breathe out love and compassion with the intention that they may be free of their heartbreak. If we're practicing for a family member who's been diagnosed with cancer, we breathe in pain and breathe out comfort for all beings who suffer from cancer, both directly and indirectly. If we're practicing on ourselves because our child has inadvertently (or intentionally) made us feel like shit, we breathe for all parents out there whose children have made them feel like shit.

That's my version of Tonglen in a nutshell. It's a practice you can use anywhere and anytime, once you're comfortable and familiar enough with it. You can derive the greatest benefit from Tonglen when you learn to use it naturally whenever a painful situation arises (either one that affects you directly, or indirectly through someone who's in any sort of pain). *This* is Everything Mind—bringing it all to the path, the light and the dark, and not just our own light and darkness, but *all* light and darkness.

I'm looking for a dare-to-be-great situation.

LLOYD DOBLER, IN *SAY ANYTHING*

GIVE ME THE UNDERDOGS

ickboxing, the sport of the future!

Okay, so while that may not have panned out for Lloyd Dobler in the classic 1989 movie *Say Anything*, John Cusack's portrayal of Dobler succeeded tenfold where kickboxing failed because it became (at least in my opinion) one of the greatest underdog stories ever told.

Never judge a book by its cover. Remember that old saying? Well, Lloyd Dobler could be that adage's poster boy. At face value, he's a goofy underachiever, but underneath his schlubby exterior is where the magic happens. Lloyd is a man of integrity and optimism, with a huge heart—an endearing mix that touched me deeply the first time I saw *Say Anything*, in my midteens.

In case you haven't seen the film (and if you haven't, do yourself a favor and watch it), the story revolves around Lloyd, who has his sights set on the class valedictorian, Diane Court. She's described as "a brain with the body of a game-show hostess," by one of his friends, who also lovingly tells Lloyd that the possibility of them becoming a couple is nothing more than a pipe dream. Lloyd refuses to be deterred, and this is where the film's most crucial theme played into my own life: believing that anything is possible.

Thanks to *Say Anything* and Lloyd's cockeyed optimism, the hackneyed "If you dream it, you can achieve it" ideology has influenced and resonated with me ever since. (Take that, *The Secret*.) I'm sure others have found similar inspiration elsewhere, possibly through sports, role models, teachers, or parents; but for me, it all began with Lloyd Dobler and his horrible, yet perfect, trench coat.

Of course I understand *Say Anything* is just a movie, so as I sat down to write this chapter, I had to ask myself a question: Why does this Hollywood story (a late-1980s one at that) still make my heart all mushy and my mind feel empowered more than twenty years later?"

Well, it's rather simple, really: because it's fucking brilliant. Who among us can't relate to the film's essential emotions: the humor, self-doubt, hope, spontaneity, and the crème de la crème of all coming-of-age tales, the dreaded fear of allowing ourselves to be vulnerable with another? All these experiences and emotions, the good and the bad, make us human. What's most important is cultivating the courage to believe in ourselves and our potential, exactly as we are in this moment, embracing our imperfectly perfect selves exactly as Lloyd did.

Joseph Campbell, author of *The Hero with a Thousand Faces*, urged us to "follow our bliss" in life. This is exemplified perfectly in Lloyd's pursuit of his own bliss: Diane Court. And while my personal bliss may not be "a brain with the body of a game-show hostess," I would travel to the ends of the earth to honor it, just like Lloyd did in *Say Anything*.

One last lesson that Lloyd Dobler taught me is that being a man—no, being a good human being—is about being brave, vulnerable, and fearless in the pursuit of our passions. So to wrap this up, allow me to share one of my favorite scenes in the film (no, not the quintessential boom-box-over-the-head scene, though of course that one is amazing too). It's at the very end of the movie, when Lloyd and Diane are on a plane headed to England (where she'll be attending school). Diane turns to Lloyd and says, "Nobody thought we would do this. Nobody thinks this will work." To which he replies, "No. But you just described every great success story."

You're goddamn right, Lloyd. I can't thank you enough for instilling that lesson—one that is still the truest of truths for me all these years later—deep in my heart and for teaching me at such a young age that inspiration can be found in the most unlikely places, including a tall, gangly, trench-coat-wearing oddball with staunch integrity and a heart of gold.

Now, I'm off to go listen to Hey Soul Classics . . . 'cause I bought my own (which won't make sense if you haven't seen *Say Anything*—so there's one more reason to go check it out).

Blessed visionary
Cut me with your sun.

MASTODON, "CRACK THE SKYE"

14

MASTODON, KING KONG,
AND INSPIRATION

ithin spiritual circles, you'll often hear the word *inspiration* equated with being "in-spirit." This means that true inspiration comes from being in alignment with our spirit, or our spiritual self. I get that. I've certainly experienced it. There have also been plenty of times throughout my journey when I've felt completely defeated and uninspired—well, spiritually speaking that is.

I've gone through periods where it seemed like no amount of meditation, mantra, or prayer was connecting me to anything deeper than that of my normal waking state. These were times when I found myself wondering if the whole spirituality thing was a sham. But thanks to the many direct experiences I'd already had that completely contradicted this frustrated thinking, I knew better. These times also reminded me that spiritual practice isn't just about basking in the bliss of peak experiences. It's also (and more importantly) about touching the present moment in whatever way it presents itself to us, embracing and working with the good times as well as the ones filled with utter shit, keeping an open heart to it all because whatever is happening in life, is the path itself—*all of it.* (Did somebody say Everything Mind?)

Spirituality is not something to be forced. It should flow through us. Inspiration works in very much the same way. The question is, once we've been doing this spirituality thing for a while, will we still be open to inspiration in all its myriad forms? Will we still be able to take a moment to look at life through an unfiltered lens, which also includes laying aside the spiritual lens? (Because after all, that's just another lens too.)

I have no problem admitting that there have been many times in the past when my head was so far up my ass with this spirituality thing that I lost sight of the fact that inspiration can strike from anywhere. I touched on this when I wrote about Lloyd Dobler, but another example of inspiration could be someone deciding to learn to play the guitar because Ian MacKaye or John Frusciante moved them. Some of you reading this had to have been inspired at some point to pick up a guitar, turn on the distortion, and rock the fuck out to songs by Minor Threat and Fugazi. Hell, maybe you just wanted to make the ladies (or men) swoon by playing them a cover of "Under the Bridge."

Regardless, inspiration is inspiration, and who knows when and how it will strike, or where it will lead? Can you imagine if Hendrix had never been inspired to pick up a guitar, or Gretzky to put on a pair of skates, or Hawk to step onto his first skateboard? Hell, maybe there's even someone out there who decided to take up acting because they thought that if Ice Cube and RZA could do it, well, so could they. (Respect of course to Ice

Cube and RZA. I'm a fan of their music . . . and acting—for the most part.)

While I've found inspiration from all the aforementioned examples, my greatest source has come from those closest to me, like my brother, who after going to a small-town high school—where the majority of the teachers were closed minded and gave the skater/alternative kids a lot of shit for no good reason—went on to become a teacher himself. He learned from his own teachers' mistakes and became the kind of educator who doesn't discriminate and actually cares about all of his students, regardless of their personal interests or style.

Then there's my mother, who, besides being a loving, supportive, and all-around incredible woman, has lived with lymphedema in her leg the majority of her life, yet still manages to get out there and walk in 5K events for various notable causes. I definitely can't leave out my father, who, besides being a loving, supportive, and all-around incredible man, was raised in foster care by a woman and her daughter, and had no male role model in his life. Yet he still managed to become one hell of an amazing parent and role model himself. (Huge props to all you single parents, male and female, out there raising your kids. Respect.)

And of course, there's my amazing wife, Jenn, who on a daily basis inspires me in countless ways, some of which include her incredibly huge heart and her tremendous creative, artistic visions and projects. Then there's the coolest thing she's ever done, which is bringing her little girl, Morgan, into this world. She is equally inspiring in her own silly, fun, curious, and loving ways.

So it's fair to say that inspiration is available to us at all times—spiritually and otherwise—as long as we're open to it. That's just my two cents. I'm intrigued by how others find inspiration, so I'll often slip that question into conversations and interviews I conduct. I've found there's never a shortage of interesting responses.

Among them, an answer that I really appreciated happened during an interview I did with Mastodon's drummer, Brann Dailor. I asked Brann from where, besides music, he drew his inspiration. He replied:

> Pretty much any and everywhere all day long. I'm big into movies and documentaries. I was actually telling this story the other day about when the King Kong remake came out, that I had to leave the theater in the middle of it to go use a payphone so I could call my house and leave a riff on the answering machine. It actually became the riff in "Crystal Skull" that Scott Kelly [of Neurosis] sings over on our *Blood Mountain* album. So it could really be anything. I'm always seeking it. I read a lot of books and look for things in the pages, a phrase that lights up which I can take and use as a jumping-off point for lyrics. I try to travel as much as I can, even when I'm home from tour. I'll go to Peru or Egypt or Russia. Thanks to my trip to Russia, I was able to finish my *Crack the Skye* story with the Rasputin thing because I became really inspired over there by all the bestial imagery and so on.[1]

Okay, so unlike Brann, we're obviously not all able to just pick up and travel to places like Peru, Egypt, and Russia; or to have completely unfamiliar sensory experiences, resulting in new, out-of-the-box inspiration. *But,* as Brann went on to explain, that's not entirely necessary to get our creative juices flowing:

> I'm always looking for it no matter where I go, keeping my eyes and ears open. You can get a riff just walking

down the street, in silence. You could be minding your own business when all of a sudden, the most beautiful noise enters your brain. And in my case, when that happens, hopefully I can guide that noise, that sound, to Bill or Brent's fingers, which then will possibly make it onto the record, resulting in the people in the crowd enjoying it. And when it all comes full circle, that chain of events happened simply because I decided to take the dog for a walk. I love that.[2]

So whether you're in Russia marveling at bestial imagery or checking out the latest blockbuster at your local theater or, hell, even simply out taking the dog for a walk, inspiration is always out there (and *in there,* thanks to Everything Mind) and often found in the most unexpected places—but only if we're open to it.

There ain't nobody to be pretty for, fuck it,
Let it rattle.

P.O.S., "LET IT RATTLE"

15

IN ALL THE WORLDS
UNTIL THE END OF TIME

So, as we've covered, inspiration is accessible in even the most unexpected and curious situations, but sometimes . . . sometimes no matter how hard you look, inspiration will seemingly be nowhere to be found, and you're going to come up empty-handed. For example, when I sit down to write, I sometimes find myself feeling completely inadequate, not only as a writer but also as someone who has anything worth saying regarding spirituality. I force out sentences that turn into paragraphs, which I then delete in serious frustration. Along with the feelings of being a shitty writer and someone who has nothing worthy to say come other self-deprecating thoughts. It's a completely uninspired experience, but I've become pretty good at reminding myself that not all hope is lost.

When I get to that state of feeling "less than," I often think about a profound teaching on—or maybe it's more accurate to say, a *guided journey* through—the experience of "I AMness" as written by Ken Wilber in his book *The Integral Vision*.

In that journey, we're guided to remember our essential I AMness, which is to say our true Self, first by noticing our present-moment awareness (which we'll go into in more detail shortly). As we anchor into the present moment, we also want to become aware of the images, thoughts, feelings, and sensations that are arising in our bodies, as well as all the objects arising around us in our environment.

So, when I'm feeling inadequate, I become aware of the complete absurdity of the mental conversation I'm having with myself. More importantly, I become conscious that, underneath the internal bickering, there is an awareness witnessing it all. For example, I acknowledge all the negative self-talk and accompanying shitty feelings as arising in my awareness instead of identifying with them. Many spiritual teachers use the example of clouds passing in the sky, saying that we're the ever-present, witnessing sky, and the clouds, temporary as they are, are our thoughts floating by.

When I feel sadness arise, instead of identifying myself with it, I identify myself with the Witnessing Awareness that is watching the sadness arise—a simple shift in perception but one that has profound effects. "I" am no longer sad but instead am aware of sadness arising within me. With awareness comes a dis-identification from the thoughts and emotions; in turn, this creates just a big-enough space to allow some peace and acceptance to enter. "I" am no longer sad, or scared, or pissed-off. Instead, I'm watching, witnessing, and acknowledging these emotions.

Going back to Ken's teaching, we next begin to think about what was in our awareness five minutes ago, noticing that most of our thoughts, sensations, and even environment may have changed. There is also something in us that is unchanged, something that is the same in this moment as it was five minutes ago. That something is what Ken calls *I AMness.*

He describes this I AMness as a "self-knowing, self-recognizing, self-validating, ever-present feeling awareness."[1] Any time I am caught in my mental ridiculousness, there is always an ever-present awareness underneath that is witnessing it all go down, with complete impartiality.

Once you've recognized that I AMness, think back to five hours ago, then to five years ago, with the understanding that countless objects, thoughts, dramas, and terrors have come, stayed a little while, and then gone. As I sat and seriously contemplated this, I thought about all the times I've judged myself, harmed myself emotionally and physically, wanted to live, wanted to die, loved God, hated God, and believed I would never return to active addiction. Through *all* these experiences, and the multitudes of others that have come and gone, the one thing that has been ever present is I AMness. It is as present right now in this very moment as it was five hours or five years ago, consistently during the good times and the bad.

We don't stop here. Our next step is to think about that which was present five centuries ago and five millennia ago. And finally, with an open heart and an open mind, to deeply contemplate the following:

All that is ever-present is I AMness. Every person feels this same I AMness—because it is not a body, not a thought, it is not an object, it is not the environment, it is not anything that can be seen, but rather is the ever-present Seer, the ongoing open and empty Witness of all that is arising, in any person, in any world, in any place, at any time, in all the worlds until the end of time, there is only and always this obvious and immediate I AMness. What else could you possibly know?[2]

When I take all this to heart, I find it really helps put into perspective just how much unnecessary suffering I have experienced—and I'm pretty sure I'm not alone in this. Why identify so rigidly with our thoughts about our temporary life circumstances and all the subsequent mental dramas they create?

Of course, there's the very reasonable chance that tomorrow, or hell, even a few hours from now, I may again fall back into some other form of drama over ridiculous shit, because at the end of the day, I'm still human. However, as I hold the teaching of I AMness close to my heart, I find that this happens significantly less often and for much shorter periods of time. It's the little victories in life, ya know?

Love sometimes wants to do us
a great favor: hold us upside down
and shake all the nonsense out.

HAFIZ

16

LOVE. SERVE. REMEMBER.

As we begin to recognize our I AMness, we learn to let go of how we think it's all supposed to be—family, friends, and work—and instead allow life to do its thing without our need to be the director in every given moment. This leads to a tremendous experience of freedom and spaciousness. Who couldn't use more of that? I'm grateful that, often, I'm actually capable of pulling this off, of stepping aside and allowing for a greater wisdom to guide me. I'd also be completely full of shit if I pretended there weren't still plenty of days that I fell entirely short as well.

In the last chapter, I mentioned how I sometimes feel inadequate as a writer, and there were certain times while I was writing this book that were no exception. I watched myself force words, feeling like I just needed to get something written rather than allow the thoughts and ideas to flow naturally. The result? Well, besides countless moments of highlighting and deleting sentences and paragraphs, I also got a bit frustrated, possibly to the point where I may have contemplated throwing my computer out of the window.

I know a part of that is because I find a false sense of security in the illusion of control. I act as if it's something tangible, something to grasp and call my own. When, of course, it's not. Sure, it feels safe and familiar, but the truth is, trying to be the director of all of life's unfoldings leaves me completely out of balance.

When I become aware that I'm trying to force things and be in control, I step back for a moment to regroup. I focus on my breath while resting in a place of both letting go and of anchoring. Then, I find myself in a place of peace and equanimity. I rest there for another moment before opening my eyes, and when I do, I generally feel much better, lighter, and more open. It's like a story Ram Dass told about a teaching his guru, Neem Karoli Baba (or Maharajji, as he was also affectionately known), gave to him while he was in India. Maharajji's teaching was to "tell the truth, love everyone, serve everyone, and remember God." Ram Dass distilled this down to "Love. Serve. Remember."—a teaching that has had a profound impact on my life.

One of the many reasons I find this teaching so important and beneficial is because it helps take me out of the director's chair and, instead, turn my focus toward the well-being of others, which, as you will see, actually includes ourselves as well.

Love (Everyone)

Okay, so at first glance you may be thinking something like, "Love everyone? Bullshit." You'd be correct, because it's virtually impossible to love everyone, especially when we're coming from the place of ego (which is where we experience most of our days). A healthy ego balances its natural instinct for self-preservation with the well-being of others. That's great; but for many of us, our ego isn't balanced. It is rooted in separation, differences, judgments, and opinions. When we're looking at life through that lens, the things we don't like about others—appearances, musical tastes, speech, mannerisms, ad infinitum—are all blatantly obvious, thus creating an imaginary boundary that closes them off from us. When we let go of being who we *think* we are, and stop labeling and judging others for who we *think* they are, then who we all *really* are shines through.

So, who are we really? We are the loving awareness that is ever present. We are I AMness. We are Everything Mind. This underlies our thoughts of who others are and who we are at all times. One way of deepening our experience of being loving awareness is to simply place our awareness in our spiritual hearts (the place in the middle of our chest we point to when addressing ourselves) and repeat to ourselves "I am loving awareness" as we go about our days, using it as a mantra that roots us. With practice, we embody this place of witnessing that is *nothing but* loving awareness so that anything entering that awareness is loved.

Ram Dass talks about his struggle with "loving everyone" while he was in India, and how Maharajji helped remedy it by saying, "Love everyone, there is only one. *Sub ek*—it's all one, just love everyone. See God everywhere. Just love everyone. Don't get angry. Ram Dass, don't get angry. Love everyone, tell the truth, love everyone, don't get angry."[1] So whether I'm watching KRS-One drop knowledge on the mic, or Sarah Palin in one of her nonsensical rants, I do my best to try to look deeper, to "see God everywhere" as Maharajji said. In a Buddhist context, we could also say: become aware of the emptiness of all things that have dependently arisen. This is Everything Mind—seeing and experiencing the interconnectedness, the Oneness, of all beings and of all thing things.

"Love everyone, there is only one." We do our best to do just that, but not in some lovey-dovey, eating sunshine and shitting rainbows kind of way. Just because we're working with a practice like loving awareness doesn't mean we're always going to feel that way. In the Suicidal Tendencies song "You Can't Bring Me Down," Mike Muir sings, "Yea maybe sometimes I do feel like shit. I ain't happy 'bout it, but I'd rather feel like shit than be full of shit!" It's not that feeling like shit is something to be glorified, but it is just as real a part of the process as the loving awareness aspect, and that's okay. It doesn't make you any less spiritual if you're feeling like shit. Actually, if you're aware that you're feeling like shit and doing something constructive to work through it, it doesn't get much more spiritual than that.

We sit in meditation and work with the "I am loving awareness" mantra. We work on seeing a piece of our self, our true Self, not only in other people, but also in the totality of life itself. Don't come down on yourself if there are times when you're not able to do it. Just be real about it and let it unfold naturally.

With dedicated practice, it gets easier; it becomes more of a natural state, and one that I can honestly say is worth spending the time to cultivate. I still fall short a lot of the time and occasionally beat myself up over it. However, the times when I am in the place of loving awareness, the place where I am able to love others unconditionally, I feel nothing short of grace personified in my life, and I wouldn't trade it for anything.

Serve (Everyone)

This one can also be tough when taken at face value, but when we remember Maharajji's words, "*Sub ek*—it's all one," this seemingly impossible task becomes much more feasible. We can start small with something as simple as a guided meditation on mindful awareness or coming home to our breath, because each moment we spend calming our minds helps connect us back to the place where everything is One. (The wonderful author and teacher Tara Brach has an extensive library of guided meditations at her website.) It's in a simple act such as this—dedicating some time out of our day to consciously come back to the place of interconnectivity with all beings—that we're serving all beings by serving our true Self.

Being of service to others in the world is just as important as "loving everyone." And I'd recommend each of us makes it a regular part of our lives. Being of service to others is also known as karma yoga, which is an important part of the spiritual path because, as we give of ourselves to others, we're simultaneously cultivating the experience of "no us" and "no them," which turns into an experience in which it's all just God serving God. I can't stress enough how powerful karma yoga can be in helping us dismantle our ego nature. Being of service to others, with an attitude of love and gratitude for nothing more than the simple fact that we're able to be of service in the first place, is a tremendously inspired and loving experience.

No matter what spiritual tradition you're a part of, being of service is a universally applicable form of spiritual practice. Hell, even if you don't give a shit about traditional spirituality in the first place, being of service simply for the benefit of humanity as a whole is huge. This is a quality inherent in most human beings, but one often dormant until called upon. For example, just look at the times when there's a natural disaster or a terrorist attack or any other number of horrors that happen on a daily basis throughout the world. What's the way most people respond? By helping. By doing whatever they can in the moment, whether it's digging people out of rubble, tending wounds, or giving away food and water. It's as if something just naturally guided them to be of service in that moment, to help others, strangers or not. I'd call that *something* Everything Mind.

The person we're working diligently to pull out of the rubble after a tornado, a tsunami, or a bombing may have been someone who, only moments earlier, we would have given the stink eye to, based on nothing more than social, political, or religious differences. In the face of disasters, tragedies, and life and death, trivial differences fly right out the window, and our instinct is to help, regardless of whether we consider ourselves spiritual or not.

In his book *The Hope,* the brilliant mystic Andrew Harvey writes:

> I respect—even revere—anyone who wants to help
> others, whatever his or her faith or lack of it. In fact, I
> have always felt a lot more at home with people who
> don't give a fig for any kind of conventional religion
> or even "spirituality," but who do something practical
> to help others, than with so-called seekers who quote
> from the Dhammapada and the "Little Flowers of Saint
> Francis" with eyes raised to heaven and do nothing to
> help anyone. As for those who use a debased and narrow
> understanding of karma or of "divine order" to justify
> doing nothing in the face of the troubles of our time, I
> have to pray for grace so as not to want to hit them on
> the head with a saucepan. Give me an atheist activist
> over a smug and passive so-called seeker any day.[2]

God bless Andrew Harvey and his wit, which he uses to make an excellent point. What good are all the spiritual practices, phrases, and niceties if we're keeping them only for ourselves or for the few people in our tribe, our sangha, our church, and so forth? There are many "nonspiritual" people out there embodying true spirituality by offering their selfless services to others, maybe even more so than people who consider themselves "spiritual" but who are focused only on self-improvement. There's nothing wrong with self-improvement, but if that's the only focus of our practice, what's really happening is that we're improving our ego's version of our spiritual self; and our ego, being the great manipulator that it is, can, and will, keep us locked in that cycle until the day we die if we allow it to.

When we are of service to others—whether it's volunteering at a soup kitchen or nursing home, speaking at a detox or rehab, or organizing food drives for those less fortunate—and doing so in the spirit of selflessness, we're taking ourselves out of the equation and, instead, merging with God's nature in all beings and things. True selfless service means you aren't doing shit. *You* are not handing a homeless person a piece of bread, God is offering God a piece of God. *Sub ek*—it's all one.

Remember (God)

Of Maharajji's teachings, I think this one is the easiest to grasp. All manifest things in life are born out of a vast, perfect, empty stillness, and thus, at their core, all share the same inherent nature. As we look out at trees, cars, animals, instruments, books, people, and highways, keeping in mind that it's all born from the same vast emptiness, we're able to see everything as an integral part and extension of God. And it's in this way of seeing that we're able to embrace God in all things and at all times, for God (as you choose to understand Him, Her, It) is just as much in a garbage can as in Christ Jesus, Henry Rollins,

Frida Kahlo, PJ Harvey, Buddha, Carrie Brownstein, Christopher Walken, Kuan Yin, Muhammad, Chuck D, Chelsea Wolfe, or Thich Nhat Hanh.

Regarding God, the Indian poet-saint Kabir wrote:

Are you looking for me? I am in the next seat.
My shoulder is against yours.
You will not find me in stupas, not in Indian shrine
rooms, nor in synagogues, nor in cathedrals:
Not in masses, nor kirtans, not in legs winding around
your own neck, nor in eating nothing but vegetables.
When you really look for me, you will see me instantly—
You will find me in the tiniest house of time.
Kabir says: Student, tell me, what is God?
He is the breath inside the breath.[3]

And after those beautifully precise words, I believe there's nothing more to say, with the exception of one final reminder that *sub ek*—it's all one or, in the spirit of this book, it's all Everything Mind.

Some crowns of sorrow sit on
a little world for a little hour.

WRENCH IN THE WORKS, "PALE FIRE"

PRACTICE

UNCONDITIONAL LOVE
AND ACCEPTANCE

It's all one, even the pain. I had to dig really deep to remind
myself of this a few years ago when my mother told me a story
about something that had happened when I was blackout drunk
at their house (which, unfortunately, wasn't the only time that
had happened). The abridged version is that, in an attempt to
keep me from harming myself or others, my father confiscated
my bottle of Klonopin (a benzodiazepine that when mixed with
alcohol makes things go from bad to worse). I was hell-bent on
getting the pills back, so what made the most sense to me in my
blackout state was to pull a large knife from their kitchen drawer,
go out to the driveway, hold the blade to my throat, and threaten
to kill myself if they didn't give me back my pills. They did.

I had absolutely no recollection of this happening, and as
I listened to my mother tell me about it, I felt my entire body

begin to tighten and my stomach tie in knots. After she finished telling me about what was a horrific experience for her and my father, I excused myself from the living room, without letting on that the story was affecting me. I didn't want to cause my mother any more pain by letting her see my own pain arising from hearing that story, because that certainly wasn't her intention and I felt like she'd already hurt enough. I headed upstairs to sit alone with the pain and emotions that were arising, and as I did, I found myself in a state that was comparable to some of the worst withdrawals I've experienced. The thought of putting a knife to my own throat and doing it in front of my mom and dad while threatening to kill myself made me sick. I sat there sweating as anxiety raced through me. Even as I'm typing these words, I feel residual uneasiness, and it *still* fucking sucks.

It was at that point—sitting there on my bed, soberly experiencing withdrawalesque symptoms—that I sought solace in a practice that is inspired by something I once heard from Thich Nhat Hanh in one of his many wisdom-filled dharma talks. He mentioned holding our painful thoughts and emotions with love in the same way a mother holds a newborn baby. The image affected me deeply. Over the course of the next several months, when painful thoughts and emotions arose, I found myself thinking about Hanh's words and began working with them, adding a few elements of my own.

I'd been working with this practice for awhile when I learned about the incident with the knife, but had not yet worked on anything quite so heavy. It was definitely scary to bring my full attention to the ridiculously shitty feelings I was experiencing as I opened my heart to the overwhelming hurt arising within. But I knew I had to do this work to release my accumulated pain.

The practice itself is relatively simple, with the exception of when we have to *actually* acknowledge and address our pain rather than act with habitual avoidance. I've broken it down into two parts for you.

Part 1

- Begin by sitting in a comfortable and stable position, spine erect but not overly rigid, belly soft, and hands placed gently in your lap in whatever way is most comfortable for you. The practice begins whenever you become aware of negative thoughts, emotions, and feelings arising, and you identify, acknowledge, honor, and accept them. Are the thoughts self-judging or are they of bad memories? How about your emotions? Even emotions as subtle as dislike or ambivalence should be taken into account. What are you feeling: depressed, angry, or anxious? Anything that causes dis-ease is applicable.

- Identify the physical sensations that are arising in you as a result of your thoughts, emotions, and feelings. Is there tightening in your chest? Is your stomach turning, or is there a throbbing sensation in your head? Again, anything that causes dis-ease is applicable.

- Once you've clearly identified the thoughts, emotions, and feelings, explore any imagery they create in your mind. Are there colors, shapes, or figures? Are they abstract or clear? (While sitting on my bed, I saw an image of spikes, like the ones the police use to stop cars, which possibly represented the extreme pain I was experiencing.) The important thing is to let the thoughts, emotions, and feelings create the imagery while you simply notice what it is. Sometimes there won't be any images and, as you'll see in the next step, that's fine.

Part 2

- So when you have the mental image of what your thoughts, emotions, and feelings have created, picture yourself holding it in the same way a mother holds a newborn baby. Picture the image wrapped in a warm blanket. If no image came to mind in the previous step, simply place your thoughts, emotions, and feelings themselves in the blanket. Now imagine yourself holding the blanket and its contents close to your chest with loving care. As you do this, imagine your heart extending unconditional love, acceptance, and compassion to the bundle. (In the beginning, if embracing the bundle of thoughts, emotions, and feelings to your chest feels too close and personal, you can also imagine wrapping them in a warm blanket, placing it in a baby carriage, and rocking it back and forth.)

- Next, mentally (or verbally) acknowledge the image, thoughts, emotions, and feelings with an open heart. Promise to care for them and to hold them with compassion for as long as they need you to, and do your best to think or say these words with sincerity.

- Finally, sit with the image, thoughts, emotions, and feelings, offering them love for as long as they need you to, until they're ready to go. I find that it usually

takes less than a minute for this to happen, but there
may be times when it takes longer (for example, I
had to sit with the pain from the knife story for
roughly half an hour).

That's the practice. We can apply it to everything from minor
stuff to our heaviest memories and most difficult experiences.
Remember that no practice is a cure-all. Sometimes, we may
need extra help from a professional, or medication, or possibly
a combination of both. And there is absolutely nothing wrong
with that. Meditation and spirituality go a long way in our healing and transformation; for some it will be all that's necessary,
but for others that won't be the case.

When we fearlessly bring our attention to the painful
thoughts, emotions, feelings, and any subsequent images that
may arise, and we tend to them with an open heart, we're doing
the most natural thing we can—expressing a pure and complete
love. It's a love they've never known before and a love many of
us have never known before either. After I sat on my bed with
an open heart and accepted the painful thoughts and emotions
while expressing love and compassion toward them, I felt as if
I'd dropped a hundred-pound weight.

So when it comes to working with, and through, difficulties,
it's all relevant; it's all grist for the mill; and it can all be healed.
Please just be as honest with yourself as possible regarding what
is and isn't working for you in said healing process, okay? It
takes a bit of willingness to lay it all out there like this, which
can be scary—trust me, I know. What I also know is that we're
all capable of doing this. We just have to decide if we'd rather
continue perpetuating the cycle of unnecessary pain or take the
power back and do something about it. So . . . what do you
want to do?

We meet ourselves time and time again
in a thousand disguises on the path of life.

CARL JUNG

17

WE ARE THE STORM

kay, so this book, or your skateboard, yoga mat, meditation cushion, all the records in your vinyl collection,
that sweet A Tribe Called Quest T-shirt you scored on eBay
(okay, that I scored on eBay) . . . you are *interbeing* with all of it.
It's *all* dependently arising on various causes and conditions that
you're an integral part of.

Thich Nhat Hanh, besides encouraging us to nurture our
painful thoughts, emotions, and feelings, also teaches exten-
sively on interbeing and the importance of understanding and
seeing it in everyday life. If you're unfamiliar with Hanh's interpretation of interbeing (or the Buddhist concept of dependent
arising), what I wrote in the previous paragraph may sound like
I'm tripping on acid or mushrooms. I assure you, those days are

well behind me (though, hey, if that's your thing, and you're doing it responsibly, rock on).

In a piece titled "What We Came For," poet Alison Luterman illuminates interbeing when she writes:

> It hit her then that every strawberry she had ever eaten—every piece of fruit—had been picked by calloused human hands. Every piece of toast with jelly represented someone's knees, someone's aching back and hips, someone with a bandanna on her wrist to wipe away the sweat. Why had no one told her about this before?[1]

So interbeing essentially means that we're completely interconnected with, and interdependent upon, every single thing, both seen and unseen in the world, and I mean *everything*. So, besides this book, you're also interbeing with the air you breathe, the food you eat, all the pretty little flowers that decorate the entire globe, as well as the baddest of badass storms that lay waste to said flowers on a daily basis. Yes indeed, just like Ron Burgundy, you're kind of a big deal. (And if you don't know who Ron Burgundy is, we can't be friends. Okay, maybe we can be friends, but you're down two cool points from the start, so go watch *Anchorman*.)

On a personal/physical level, this interbeing is pretty obvious; our bodies contain our kidneys, heart, lungs, and all the other organs and strange inner workings that rely on one another (or are interbeing with one another) to keep us alive. In addition, there are our five sense receptors—sight, taste, touch, smell, and hearing—all of which are interbeing or communicating (mostly via our brains) throughout the day. Understanding this simple view of interbeing on a strictly individual and subjective level is a step, but don't forget that interbeing includes the sum total of the entire universe, and not just our individual physical selves.

Now I know I just told you a paragraph ago that you're a pretty big deal, and I assure you, you are; but the "you" that you think you are, which is to say your body and its accompanying perceptions, isn't the entire story. A lot of shit had to happen not only in order for you to come into existence, but also for the universe as a whole. All that has arisen has done so based on causes, conditions, and effects interbeing with one another. This incredible process is all arising within the awareness of our Everything Mind.

To share a simple example of interbeing and cause and effect, let's use an acorn (cause), which grows into an oak tree (effect), and it does so because environmental factors such as sunlight, soil, and rain (conditions) are adequate. That's just one very basic example. Interbeing (or dependent arising) relates to anything in the physical world because *all things* that exist depend on other factors; therefore *anything* and *everything* is empty of independent existence, and instead is *interbeing* with everything else.

Thich Nhat Hanh's teaching is a wonderful tool for cultivating greater compassion for all beings because meditating on it leads to deepening our understanding and experience of the interconnectivity we share with all life. Contrary to what our egos tell us, we are not just separate, isolated beings, housed strictly in our physical bodies. Instead, we're an integral part of life's unfolding, which goes as far back as the big bang. As astrophysicist Neil deGrasse Tyson said:

> Recognize that the very molecules that make up your body, the atoms that construct the molecules, are traceable to the crucibles that were once the centers of high-mass stars that exploded their chemically rich guts into the galaxy, enriching pristine gas clouds with the

chemistry of life. So that we are all connected: to each other biologically, to the earth chemically, and to the rest of the universe atomically. That's kinda cool! That makes me smile, and I actually feel quite large at the end of that. It's not that we are better than the universe; we are part of the universe. We are in the universe, and the universe is in us.[2]

That's pretty inspiring, yet at the same time quite humbling, right? Our interconnectedness with life really doesn't get much clearer than that.

I'll share another example of interbeing and dependent arising based on an experience I had a few years ago while covering a Motörhead/Slayer concert for my website theindiespiritualist. com. (Shameless plug—*what?*) I had a nifty photo pass that gave me access to the area directly in front of the stage (lucky me, I know). So there I was, standing up front waiting for Motörhead to come on, when all of a sudden the stage went dark, and the sound of a guitar being plugged in ripped through the PA system. The crowd began to go crazy, and chants of "MOTÖRHEAD!" roared throughout the stadium. Fifteen seconds later, the lights came back on, and there, standing roughly a foot in front of me, was greatness himself, Motörhead's bassist/singer . . . Lemmy-fucking-Kilmister!

I've covered a lot of shows and interviewed a lot of bands—and actors, comedians, spiritual teachers (it's part of my job)—and rarely do I get that caught up in the whole star-struck thing, but this was Lemmy, a metal god among gods. An interesting thing happened roughly a minute into Motörhead's first song (after getting over my fanboy nerd-out, of course), when I noticed Lemmy's Rickenbacker bass. It was a model I hadn't seen him play before, and it was insanely gorgeous. It had an all-natural wood finish complemented by a beautiful, hand-carved leaf inlay that covered the entire body of the instrument.

As I was standing there in awe of Lemmy's bass, my mind naturally gravitated toward the teachings of interbeing (spiritual nerd problems, I suppose) and I began thinking about how his bass—before becoming the instrument of a metal god—was first a part of a tree. As I thought about that tree, my thoughts then turned to the sun, and how without its nurturing rays, the tree wouldn't have been able to grow in the first place. Of course it wasn't just sunshine that fostered the tree's growth—there had to be oxygen, and rain, and soil. Going a step further, I contemplated the fine artisans at Rickenbacker who made the bass, and the equipment in their shop they used to make it. Then I thought about the workers themselves, and how it was thanks only to their parents that they were born in the first place.

So, while I was standing there admiring Lemmy's amazingly badass instrument, I saw everything that had to *inter-be* for the Rickenbacker to have made its way into Lemmy's hands. It didn't end there. I continued thinking about how the same sunshine, clouds, and rain that had to inter-be for the tree to grow so it could birth Lemmy's bass also had to inter-be in order for the food to grow that you and I, and hell, even Lemmy, eat on a daily basis. (Though, truth be told, I've often pictured Lemmy as someone who eats car engines rather than actual food.)

So to bring this full circle, what had begun only moments earlier as Motörhead ripping into their first song of the night culminated in my experience of interbeing and dependent arising as illuminated through Lemmy Kilmister's bass guitar. Everything was all right there—the trees, sunshine, clouds, rain, you, me, Lemmy, and the universe as a whole—all interbeing with one another and coming to fruition in Lemmy's bass. Oh, and seriously, I wasn't on any hallucinogens.

You are an aperture through which the universe is looking at and exploring itself.

ALAN WATTS

PRACTICE

INNER BODY AWARENESS

If we wish to make any significant changes or progress in life, we always have to start from the inside out, and cultivating our experience of interbeing is no exception. It is equally important to be familiar both with the interbeing that's happening internally (formlessness) as well as externally (form). The practice of inner body awareness can lay a very strong foundation for doing this. Spiritual teacher Eckhart Tolle has often talked about it in his books and workshops (though I'm sure its origins trace back farther than him). In case you're not completely familiar with the "inner body," here are a few words from Tolle to help clarify:

> Your inner body is not solid but spacious. It is not your physical form but the life that animates the physical form. It is the intelligence that created and sustains

the body, simultaneously coordinating hundreds of different functions of such extraordinary complexity that the human mind can only understand a tiny fraction of it. When you become aware of it, what is really happening is that the intelligence is becoming aware of itself. It is the elusive "life" that no scientist has ever found because the consciousness that is looking for it *is it*.[1]

That's just a brief description, but one I believe is of great service for us to understand before going deeper into this practice. It helps us (in real time) to become intimate with the life energy that gives rise to and sustains our material existence, which is to say the energy that bridges the *seeming* gap between the worlds of form and formlessness.

The practice itself is quite simple, but don't let that fool you into underestimating its effects.

- Start by closing your eyes and taking a few conscious breaths. (Closing your eyes is not always necessary, and the more you do the practice, the more easily you'll be able to do it anytime and anywhere—eyes opened or closed.)

- Next, become aware of the air you're breathing. Pay attention to it as it enters your body on the in-breath and leaves your body on the out-breath.

- Once you feel grounded in this breathing (usually two or three conscious breaths are enough), turn your attention inward and see if you can begin to feel, or sense, your inner body.

- (I've found the easiest place to begin bringing attention is the hands—so let's start there.) Bring your attention to your fingertips and, within a few seconds, you *should* begin to feel a slight tingling sensation. Once you do, slowly bring your attention down from your fingertips, through the rest of your fingers, and become *aware* of your hands in their entirety.

- Remember, don't *think* about your fingers and hands; rather, just place your attention there. Allow the tingling sensation—the aliveness within your hands—to grow and intensify.

- Hold your attention there for another moment or two (or three—just go with what feels natural) and, once you feel anchored into the aliveness of your hands, allow that internal energy—the tingling aliveness—to expand from your hands into your forearms. Keep your awareness in your forearms until you feel the aliveness both there and in your hands, and once you feel anchored in both, bring your awareness into your upper arms, repeating the previous steps.

- From there, do the same from your upper arms into your chest, and then into your abdomen, legs, feet, and head (in whatever order feels right to you) until you're aware of the aliveness in, and throughout, your entire body. Now, sit with this for as long as feels meaningful. It may be five minutes, or it may be an hour. You'll know what's right for you.

As I mentioned, you can practice this anytime and anywhere, so even if you do it only for a few minutes at a time, that's totally fine. It's a versatile practice that works when you're sitting quietly at home, when you're stuck in traffic (with your eyes open, of course), in a long line at the bank, or especially when you're in a long-ass, boring meeting and feeling like you want to claw your eardrums out. Regardless, it's an excellent practice for helping to take the focus from your discursive thoughts and to mindfully go within instead.

There's tremendous peace to be found in this practice. As we bring our attention to our inner body, we're tuning into the creative play of life that's happening within—and interconnecting every one of us on a very deep level. We're becoming more intimate with the absences of separation between form and formlessness, and this is what allows us to experience the interbeing of *every single thing!* (We'll continue to go deeper into Thich Nhat Hanh's teaching on this—and more—in the next chapter.) That's got to be better than allowing ourselves to drift on autopilot, stuck in the cyclic thoughts and emotions that are revolving around whatever we're not psyched about in the moment, right? Obviously it's your call, but I'm just sayin' . . .

Art and love are the same thing:
it's the process of seeing yourself
in things that are not you.

CHUCK KLOSTERMAN

IN PIECES

efore stumbling into this whole writing thing, I worked
as an assistant site director for a before- and after-
school enrichment program for elementary school kids and was
inspired by the children on a daily basis. Sure, kids will be kids,
and there were plenty of difficult days that left me questioning
my sanity, particularly when all they wanted to do was have
a dance party and blast Selena Gomez, Katy Perry, and Justin
Bieber. I still get shivers just thinking about it, but in retrospect,
I wouldn't trade any of it (well, minus the horrible music) for
the world.

I found myself most fascinated by the kindergarteners' and
first and second graders' unfiltered sense of wonder toward life
in general. Watching the children become captivated by simple
magic tricks, their excitement when stumbling across a new kind

of bug on the playground, or the joy they'd emanate while play-ing one of their favorite games in the gym always left me—in a vicarious way—excited and mesmerized too.

I'd usually show up to work with the other staff members around a quarter to seven in the morning, and we'd set up the room with various games, arts and crafts, and other stations for the kids to choose from. We would typically change things up each day, but there were a few staples we made sure were avail-able to the kids on a regular basis. One of them was the Lego station, which a lot of the kids tended to go ape-shit over.

I enjoyed watching their inspired imaginations as they cre-ated things like fortresses, spaceships, boats, houses, and castles, all of which started from nothing more than a big bucket of mishmashed pieces from a plethora of different sets, and all without instructions. Once the morning session was over, the kids would toss their meticulously crafted masterpieces back into the bucket, usually pausing a moment to enthusiastically watch them smash apart, and then off to school they'd go.

Now, you may be asking yourself, "What the hell does this have to do with anything . . . especially spirituality?"

As I mentioned in the introduction, one of the fundamen-tal teachings of Buddhism that is extremely beneficial for anyone to study, regardless of their spiritual tradition (or lack thereof), is emptiness, or śūnyatā. As humans, we have the tendency to create conceptual labels for, well, pretty much everything, both good and bad. Before we started naming, judging, praising, and damning things, it all just was as it was (and still, in this very moment, simply is as it is). So we give these people, places, and things labels, believing they have their own inherent existence when, in fact, they don't. Remember interbeing: all things are dependently arising in relation to one another, from our inner subjective selves to the outer objective world, and thus, it is all empty of an intrinsic and independent existence. Thich Nhat Hanh builds on this concept when he explains:

> Because form is emptiness, form is possible. In form we find everything else—feelings, perceptions, mental formations, and consciousness. "Emptiness" means empty of a separate self. It is full of everything, full of life. The word "emptiness" should not scare us. It is a wonderful word. To be empty does not mean to be nonexistent. . . . Emptiness is the ground of everything. "Thanks to emptiness, everything is possible." That is a declaration made by Nagarjuna, a Buddhist philosopher of the second century. Emptiness is quite an optimistic concept. If I am not empty, I cannot be here. And if you are not empty, you cannot be there. Because you are there, I can be here. This is the true meaning of emptiness. Form does not have a separate existence.[1]

There you have it, straight from the pen of one of our most important contemporary spiritual teachers. How truly inspiring is it to know that thanks to emptiness, everything is possible? Those infinite impossibilities apply to you, to me, to every sentient being, and to the entire goddamn universe. *Miraculous!*

People often misunderstand the teachings on emptiness and think of it as something nihilistic when that couldn't be further from the truth. Emptiness in relation to ourselves simply means that we're actually empty of an individual, intrinsic self. It does not mean that there's no "being" here experiencing life, because obviously, you're reading these words right now, aren't you? It's just that the "you" that you think is reading these words—as an inherent, separate self—actually isn't. All this, from believing we're inherently separate to then recognizing that we're not and instead are interbeing with all things, is happening within the realm of Everything Mind.

The Buddha teaches that the totality of life, including everything we experience, comes into being as a result of causes and conditions. It's through understanding this that we clearly see the interdependent nature of literally *every single thing* and how everything depends on something else—other elements and factors—in order to originate in the first place.

This awareness is the first step in breaking our deeply rooted conditioning of living life from a place identified strictly with our physical being and sense perceptions. We then begin to break away from the idea of a separate, inherent self, seeing the emptiness of all phenomena, which the Buddha taught was essential for liberation and being released from suffering.

Once we really begin to contemplate this, I think most of us would be hard-pressed to refute what the Buddha taught. As His Holiness the Fourteenth Dalai Lama explains:

> Buddha teaches that the very fact that something is
> dependently originated means that it is necessarily
> devoid of an essential, or independent, reality.
> For if something is fundamentally dependent, by
> logical necessity it must be devoid of having a
> nature that is independent of other phenomena,
> of existing independently. Thus it is said that
> anything that is dependently originated must also
> be, in actual fact, empty.[2]

This leads us to the Buddha's teaching on emptiness as found in the famous scripture the Heart Sutra, the following excerpt of which shares the essence of the teaching:

Avalokiteshvara Bodhisattva,
doing deep Prajña Paramita
clearly saw emptiness
of all the five conditions
thus completely relieving
misfortune and pain.
Oh Shariputra, form is no other
than emptiness,
emptiness no other than form.
Form is exactly emptiness,
emptiness exactly form.
Sensation, conception,
discrimination, awareness
are likewise like this.
Oh Shariputra, all dharmas
are forms of emptiness;
not born, not destroyed,
not stained, not pure,
without loss, without gain.
So in emptiness there is no form;
no sensation, conception,
discrimination, awareness;
no eye, ear, nose, tongue,
body, mind;
no color, sound, smell, taste,
touch, phenomena;
no realm of sight,
no realm of consciousness,
no ignorance
and no end to ignorance,
no old age and death
and no end to old age and death,

no suffering, no cause of suffering,
no extinguishing, no path,
no wisdom, and no gain.
No gain and thus the Bodhisattva
lives Prajna Paramita,
with no hindrance in the mind;
no hindrance, therefore no fear.
Far beyond deluded thoughts;
this is Nirvana.[3]

The Heart Sutra teaches that it's thanks to emptiness that we are not isolated beings and can deeply touch and experience the place where we're interbeing with all life. Even simply recognizing the fact that each of us depends on one another is a huge service to all beings. That, in and of itself, is a step in the direction of unity rather than separation, and in awakening Everything Mind. Contemplating that others are responsible for growing the food we eat, constructing the buildings we meditate or pray in, making the clothes we wear, treating us for sickness and physical ailments helps us to realize that without their services, we wouldn't be able to stay alive.

Everything that we know today—from useless trivia to the knowledge we've accumulated from the great wisdom traditions, from our artistic and musical abilities to cooking, snowboarding, yoga—we've learned from someone else. And as we become clearer on just how dependent upon and interconnected with others we truly are, the more organically we begin to extend kindness and compassion. As our spiritual practice (whatever it may be) grows deeper, it becomes clear that "us" and "them" are nothing more than concepts we've been taught to give others and ourselves. We are in this thing together, and the sooner we become clear on that, the sooner we will become friendlier toward life, and life toward us.

Okay, so that's nice and all but . . . *what about those damn Legos?* I'm getting to that, I promise, but first, I need to mention my love for running, as that too plays a part in the equation.

At the time when I was working at the school program, I would go out for daily jogs. I started noticing myself looking at my surroundings—the trees, cars, people, buildings, houses, animals, and so forth—in relation to the Buddhist teachings on emptiness and dependent arising, but in a way that was similar to how the children created their Lego masterpieces.

As I ran, I would imagine the house scattered across the yard in separate pieces, similar to the heap of Lego pieces before the kids got to them and started building. I'd see the wood in one area; the sinks, tubs, and toilets in another; the nails, paint, and siding in yet another, and . . . you get the picture. Just like watching the kids build with Legos, I'd envision all the pieces of the house coming together. Rather than seeing the house as having its own independent nature, I could now understand it as it truly was: in a state of dependent arising. All those pieces, the wood, nails, sinks, and toilets, came together in order for the house to be a house.

Now, that's a manufacturing example. I would also do this with people and animals. For example, I would see someone working in their yard and mentally break them down, envisioning their arms in one area, legs in another, head here, and internal organs there. Then I would picture it all coming back together, culminating in the person once again, a complete being working on their yard.

Yes, I understand this may sound a bit crazy, but it really is the nature of how things are in life; everything is dependently arising. When we begin to understand this, we experience tremendous liberation from suffering because we're able to see that things really aren't as personal or subjective as we make them.

When we look deeper into phenomena, we see their true nature as part of the great indivisible body of reality. We see that nothing exists separately from anything else. We free ourselves from rigid conceptualization and categorization. Of course, concepts, labels, categories, and so forth play a major role in the basic functioning of our day-to-day lives and they're obvious necessities, but now we're able to also see beyond their limitations. Sure, we can see that a table is a table by name and function, but looking deeper, we can also see that it has no intrinsic "tableness" to it. We still see the table, but now we're able to see past the illusion of its separate, inherent existence, noticing that it consists of four legs, a top, nails, and so forth, all of which have to come together to make it a "table" in the first place.

This applies to *everything*. We can learn to see things exactly as they are, not as we've named and judged them to be. When we look at things through our judgments and concepts, the universe appears as *samsara*—an illusion. Once we're free of our judgments and conceptualizations, we see that everything is no longer separate or isolated. Instead, it's completely interconnected as One, as ISness, as the ground of all being, as emptiness, as our inherent nature that *unites us all.*

Eventually, when we've become rooted in a place that's free of labels and conceptualizations, we may find this teaching frees us from the *concepts* of interbeing and impermanence altogether. These concepts are wonderful tools to work with, but we want to be careful not to become dependent on them. To again draw from the wisdom of Thich Nhat Hanh:

> These kinds of concepts are exactly what the Buddha
> said we should get rid of. He said that nirvana is the
> complete extinction of concepts, including the concepts
> of impermanence and nonself. When you want to start

a fire, you light a match, and then the fire consumes the match. The teachings of impermanence and nonself are like the match. If you practice with intelligence and succeed in your practice, the match will be consumed and you will be completely free.[4]

So my friends, set it on fire, watch it burn, and rejoice in the ashes of liberation. This is your true freedom.

So let's go out west and bask in the overcast
And walking through the rain we'll see the
beauty in life again.

DARKEST HOUR, "WITH A THOUSAND WORDS TO SAY BUT ONE"

PRACTICE

THE FIVE REMEMBRANCES

Growing old, getting sick, dying—loss and impermanence are very painful realities, and we have to inter-be with it all. However, if we're truly honoring the path that brings *everything* to the table—to the Everything Mind—then it's up to us to be responsible for our actions. That's where the Five Remembrances come in. They're a teaching in the Upajjhatthana Sutta, part of Buddhism's Pali Canon. It's something the Buddha suggested practitioners do each morning in an effort to make peace with sicknesses of varying kinds as well as old age and inevitable death (not forgetting that only our relative material selves die, whereas our I AMness, our ultimate ever-present Self, is beyond mortality). Reciting the Five Remembrances each morning in a way that's truly contemplative—taking to heart what we're actually saying—can ultimately free us of our worldly longings, which in turn allows us to appreciate life without attachment to it. Yeah, I know that may sound bleak, but I promise you that if you regularly recite these words, you'll experience deeper insight and freedom. The nature of the teaching of the Five Remembrances is always the same, though the wording of some translations varies. In keeping with the Thich Nhat Hanh theme, here's his version:

1. I am of the nature to grow old. There is no way to escape growing old.
2. I am of the nature to have ill-health. There is no way to escape having ill-health.
3. I am of the nature to die. There is no way to escape death.
4. All that is dear to me and everyone I love are of the nature to change. There is no way to escape being separated from them.
5. My actions are my only true belongings. I cannot escape the consequences of my actions. My actions are the ground on which I stand.[1]

Working with the Five Remembrances has really helped me make peace with the "darker" side of my Everything Mind. The part where I truly accept that nothing lasts forever and that, with each moment that passes, I'm one moment closer to death. I don't live my life consumed with thoughts of dying. I do my very best to live each day to the fullest because after all I've been through, each day really is a gift. In order to live fully each day, I can't ignore the darkness or the light, the things that aren't very pleasant to think about and the things that are.

I love my wife and daughter in a way that I recognize borders on attachment, which Buddhism teaches is a root cause of suffering. If I were to lose either one of them—I don't have words for how I would feel. My wife and I both have very odd senses of humor and will occasionally joke about how we each want to be the first to die (when we're older, not any time soon) because we don't want to suffer the pain of losing the other. We joke about this, but I know there's truth underlying our playful exchange. The Five Remembrances haven't magically made me feel like I'd be fine were I to lose my loved ones—they're not supposed to do that. What they have done is help me to cultivate some semblance of acceptance that death is one of the realities in life, because aversion is futile, and, indeed, my actions are my only true belongings.

> Those who insist they've got their "shit together"
> are usually standing in it at the time.

STEPHEN LEVINE

19

THE "END OF MY ROPE" IS A NOOSE

Taking a sincere no-bullshit look at our mortality along with ourselves and our past actions can definitely be an uncomfortable and often embarrassing endeavor. The thing is, touching these places is what we need to do if we want to really get on with our healing, reconnect with our inherent basic goodness, and remember our fundamental nature as open, empty, and free. That's why the last few chapters shared at length the Buddhist teachings on dependent arising and emptiness—they help us to directly touch our spacious and free Self, our Everything Mind. It's from that place of emptiness that we can look directly at ourselves—our mortality, our fuck-ups, and all the places we fall short in life—with compassion and fearlessness, recognizing that none of it is as personal as we'd believed. From our ego's perspective, this sounds completely counterintuitive because, as far as the ego is concerned, we are nothing more than our physical body, its sense perceptions, its past (and present) actions, and *especially* its mortality. As we go deeper into our understanding and experience of emptiness and dependent arising, we're able see past this illusion and take a much lighter approach to working through the things we previously avoided because they seemed too painful and embarrassing.

One of the best attitudes we can cultivate during this process is the ability to laugh at some of our past screwups—especially for those of us who have really been through the wringer. Roshi Bernie Glassman and actor Jeff Bridges wrote a wonderful book titled *The Dude and the Zen Master,* in which Bernie offers a simple practice to help us break up the seriousness we place on life and all its myriad situations and experiences—both good and bad. Bernie writes: "Wake up in the morning, go to the bathroom, pee, brush your teeth, look in the mirror, and laugh at yourself. Do it every morning to start off the day, as a practice."[1]

I'm so glad I came across that practice because I can't even begin to tell you how much time I've spent berating myself over things like the emotional harm I caused others during the years of my active addiction. But really, what good does negative self-talk like that do for anyone? Learning to laugh at ourselves and life a little bit more can really go a long way in helping us to take things easier. It took quite some time for me to break that cycle—the negative self-talk and overly serious attitude about life—but I finally realized all the energy I was putting into berating myself could be used for actually effecting positive change in the world (if even only on a very small scale). I came to terms with the fact that there is nothing I can do to change my past, but *what I could do* is put my energy into living the best life I can today, being of service wherever possible, and learning to bring compassion and levity to unpleasant past memories when they arise.

This shift has helped me let go of so much needless suffering. Of course, there are still some extremely dark times, the ones that I'll never be able to laugh at, much less make some semblance of peace with. But like most people who are recovering from addiction or (as I quoted Father Keating as saying in the introduction) from "the human condition," I'm left with at least a few ridiculous memories.

Something that comes to mind happened during my early twenties. My closest drinking friend and I had finally begun to admit to ourselves that we had a problem. No catastrophic event led us to this realization. We'd just gotten exceptionally sick of ourselves and how shitty our day-to-day existence had become: wake up, hit the liquor store, go to work, take a break to sneak some drinks and snort some pills (usually Ritalin to stay focused and energized), hit another liquor store at lunch, take another break for drinks and pills, finish work, go home, drink more, sometimes band practice and sometimes not, either way drink until passing out, and repeat.

My friend and I had actually attended a 12-step meeting a few months before coming to terms with our problem, but we were (of course) half in the bag when we went. After sitting there for the first forty-five minutes, we decided we weren't nearly as bad off as the others in the room and decided to take off. Yes, this from two people who needed a drink to go to a 12-step meeting in the first place.

So having attended that one meeting and deciding that it wasn't for us, we figured we'd take matters into our own hands. Our brilliant idea? Well, it was more of a collaborative, two-pronged approach. We knew that we had to replace the alcohol with some other drink (this was well before the Red Bull/Monster energy-drink craze, which I'm sure we would have opted for had it been available at the time), so we decided that Kool-Aid, yes, Kool-Aid, would be our saving grace. Why Kool-Aid? Well, our rationale was that the sugary goodness would be enough to satisfy our urges for alcohol. As for the second part of our two-pronged approach? Marijuana. We had no interest in actually being sober per se, but rather just not drinking anymore. As far as we were concerned, weed was natural (which, sure, it is), plus we'd already been smoking it for years and hadn't had any major issues as a result, so it *couldn't* have been bad for us.

So there we were, smoking weed and drinking Kool-Aid, and we bullshitted ourselves into believing that this ridiculous method would work. And it did . . . for all of two days before we went back to drinking. Since we had accomplished such a magnificent feat of abstinence, to celebrate we decided to add sniffing heroin to our repertoire . . . and so it went.

Now I'm not here to debate whether marijuana, or even alcohol for that matter, is "bad" for an individual, because only you know what's right for you. If you suffer from the disease of addiction, as my friend and I do, then drinking any type of alcohol or smoking pot and thinking it's not an issue is something you may want to reconsider. The saying "A drug is a drug is a drug" is popular among recovering addicts for a reason. Replacing one drug for another—alcohol for heroin, or pot for alcohol—may work for a few days (or even months), but it's been shown time and again by sad and often tragic examples that we're inevitably going to return to our drug of choice and end up right back where we left off the last time we were using (and that's the best-case scenario).

I have friends who are able to drink and/or do certain drugs recreationally, and that works for them, so who am I to judge? I just know that in my and many other addicts' experience, there is no middle ground. I'd be full of shit if I said there weren't times when I wish there were. I don't romanticize using, but there are certainly occasions when a drink sounds great, or a joint, or dropping out of "reality" for a bit on an acid or mushroom trip. But I've learned through several relapses that it just doesn't work like that for me. And the same can be said for those who turn to any sort of external distraction—food, shopping, video games—to try to mask whatever pain they'd rather not feel. Avoiding pain through acts of aversion does no one any good because they only keep the pain suppressed, and that's the shit that wreaks havoc on our insides, causing stress, anxiety, depression, and so many other unnecessary and awful experiences.

Today, I use my occasional fleeting thoughts about how nice it'd be to get fucked-up as a reminder of the times when I *did* act on them and how that landed me in jails, emergency rooms, and psych hospitals. So it's in gratitude that now I have a sound-enough mind to sincerely take that into consideration and, after doing so, simply say *No fucking way* to going back down that road. Not today.

Freedom is the will to be responsible to ourselves.

FRIEDRICH NIETZSCHE

PRACTICE

CHECK YOURSELF

One way I keep myself from going back down the road of addiction is with a practice I call "checking myself." The tenth step of the 12-step fellowships states, "We continued to take personal inventory and when we were wrong promptly admitted it." This step is not only applicable for those in recovery, but really for anyone with a pulse. Taking a personal inventory means taking an honest look at ourselves: our actions, attitudes, and the way we treat people (including ourselves) on a daily basis.

The practice itself is simple and consists of taking a few moments each night before going to bed to mentally review our day. We take an honest and fearless look at our behaviors, actions, reactions, and most importantly, our motives. When we find something that we know we could have handled better, we own it. We make the proper amends as soon as possible. Our amends don't need to be grand gestures. They can be as simple as letting the other person know that we were in the wrong, that it was our bad, and that we're sorry.

Those in recovery may need to be a little more thorough while practicing this step because, as most recovering addicts probably know, the disease will use *anything,* including seemingly minor and insignificant guilt over our past actions, to its advantage. Even for those of us who aren't addicts, the voice in our heads still loves to play the blame game. So why give it the chance when it's just as easy to own our mistakes and make good with the person we offended or treated in a shitty way? This practice can be beneficial for anyone who applies it. Early on in my own recovery from addiction, a huge part of my process was to offer my sincere apologies and regrets to those I'd harmed, from girlfriends I wasn't mentally or emotionally there for to family and friends whom I'd put through emotional hell, and many more. Saying a sincere and heartfelt "I'm sorry" can be very healing for *everyone* involved in our lingering messed-up life situations.

These days, this practice has gone on to become an organic part of my life, recovery oriented or not. I've found that using the various practices I share with you in this book has helped me to live from a place where I'm much more aware of my words and behavior toward others—because as I've mentioned, I'm human and still have plenty of faults. What's interesting, however, is that since checking myself has become such an integral part of my life, any time I have been in the wrong with someone else but haven't owned it, I experience an urgency to right that wrong no matter what story my ego is saying about who *is* right or wrong. (Just ask my wife.) From my work with making amends, I know that I have the choice to experience peace rather than allow pride to dictate my well-being.

The best part of this practice is that all it takes is a few moments! You can even do it every few days if that's what feels right for you. Being proactive in our own healing and growth benefits all beings because, when we're coming from a stronger mental and emotional place, we're offering all of life our best possible self. What more could anyone ask for?

> God damn, homey, my mind is playing tricks on me.

20

AT THE MOUNTAIN OF MADNESS

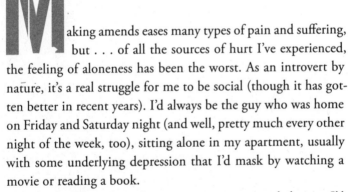

Making amends eases many types of pain and suffering, but . . . of all the sources of hurt I've experienced, the feeling of aloneness has been the worst. As an introvert by nature, it's a real struggle for me to be social (though it has gotten better in recent years). I'd always be the guy who was home on Friday and Saturday night (and well, pretty much every other night of the week, too), sitting alone in my apartment, usually with some underlying depression that I'd mask by watching a movie or reading a book.

Some nights, when the emptiness was overwhelming, I'd take a walk in the hopes of passing a few people, simply to feel like I wasn't alone, even if for only that brief second or two as they passed me by. If that didn't do the trick, I'd go home and eat some unhealthy food (pizza or chocolate-flavored anything) to get the relief I was desperately seeking. That was, of course, unless it was during one my various periods of active addiction, in which case I'd just get shitfaced, swallow pills, write angry journal entries to God, drunk-dial people, and all sorts of other ridiculous behavior.

Drunk, fucked-up, alone, depressed, or whatever, I still managed to stick with my spiritual practices (mostly meditation, prayer, and mantra) through those years. Of course, they weren't having too much of an impact because, more often than not, I was doing them just to feel like I was making some kind of effort to try to better myself. But it wasn't all a waste of time. As a result of my practice, I definitely had some transcendent experiences—ones that gave me a glimpse into the more friendly, calm, and peaceful life that I could have but wasn't quite ready for yet.

The big takeaway for me was that, once I began having even these minor tastes of awakening, of experiencing the interconnectivity, the interbeing of all things, it became clear to me that my greatest source of suffering was rooted in my sense of separation—and not just from others, but from the totality of life.

It's easy to write all this off as some esoteric nonsense because sure, on the relative, manifest level, you're you and I'm me. If I die, odds are that you probably won't as a result. I can easily grab my skateboard, set it on fire, watch it burn to ash; yet my life will still go on even though the skateboard's existence ceases to be. This is all true on the material level; however, we often overlook another part of our existence: the absolute, formless, *unmanifest* level—the place of perfect and complete Oneness. So complete in fact, that even the idea of separation doesn't exist there, only emptiness.

In the spirit of clarity, let's take a deeper look at this. On the one hand, we have *relative* or *conventional* truth, which is our everyday material experience of the world; on the other hand, we have the *absolute* or *ultimate* truth, which is the ground of all things before they manifest. These two truths—or two levels of reality—are not separate. They are completely and simultaneously coexisting with one another, and together make up Everything Mind. It's like the Zen sutra Sandokai (The Identity of Relative and Absolute) teaches, "Ordinary life fits the absolute like a box and its lid."[1]

Relative truth is the level of form (physical, psychological, and physiological), and it's where we enter the spiritual path. It's where our passion for truth is ignited, by way of any number of material things such as the texts from the great wisdom traditions, workshops, retreats, nature, performing or listening to music, losing ourselves in the act of making love, meditating—anything that fans our hearts' flames. These doorways lead us back home to the ultimate experience—a nonexperience or pure nonduality—of who we truly are as timeless, formless, complete bliss, and perfection.

The relative level is also where we spend so much time suffering unnecessarily because many of us live with rigid and concrete concepts about reality, rather than letting them all go and actually experiencing reality itself, free of preconceived notions. Much easier said than done, but doable nonetheless. It's not going to happen overnight, though (unless you've got some stellar karma built up). If we look back at our lives, particularly our formative years, it's pretty easy to see that we've been conditioned by society, our parents, teachers, and friends to identify with our material selves—our names, socioeconomic positions, bodies, sense perceptions. I'm not trying to bash society or anyone else, because they were simply teaching and instilling in us what was taught to and instilled in them. For the most part, they did so believing it was in our best interests (which in many cases it most certainly was, like not touching the stove when it's hot or getting into a stranger's van when they offer you candy).

As a result of identifying primarily—if not exclusively—with our relative selves, we've spent so much of our lives living from a place of separation, personalizing the stories our thoughts create about our material selves. Then we identify with the emotions our thoughts produce, believing that's the totality of our experience, which leads to living in aloneness, as singular, isolated beings.

When we live from that place, we're not aware that there's more than relative truth (form); and for many of us, the absolute truth (formlessness) of our experience goes by completely unnoticed. We're not in touch with what the Hindu tradition calls the *atman*, the indwelling Spirit that stirs within us. It's this disconnect—this place of forgetfulness—where our experience of fear, pain, and suffering arises. When we completely identify with the physical realm—the world—we're relying on *impermanent* things to fulfill our internal desire to find peace and refuge. But life doesn't work like that.

As we take a deeper look into the nature of the relative, the world of form, we begin to see the interconnectivity of all things, which depersonalizes much of our life experience (in a good way that creates freedom from the suffering that results from attachment and aversion). This becomes a gateway for us to enter into the experience of ultimate truth—that the objects "out there" aren't really out there, but rather they're "in here," in our awareness of them as they arise. The totality of life is arising within our awareness. So ultimately speaking, we are not in the world; the world is *in* us, it is occurring *in* our Witnessing Awareness. (But more on that later.)

There's a Sanskrit phrase, *neti-neti*, which means "not this, not that." When it comes to cultivating our experience of ultimate truth, this practice of negation is exceptionally helpful. Traditionally, neti-neti refers to things like our body, name, senses, and thoughts. As we dis-identify from these as the be-all and end-all of who we are, we find that the only thing left is emptiness, the ground of *ultimate* reality, the place of pure, infinite Spirit.

There is another saying, from the ancient Hindu text Chandogya Upanishad, which can also be extremely helpful in coming to experience the ultimate truth. It is *tat tvam asi,* and means "thou art that." Sounds contradictory to neti-neti, right? In actuality, it's not. Each is addressing a different level of reality. Neti-neti is used on the relative level to negate all material things as the totality of who we are. Whereas tat tvam asi is used on the absolute level, saying that you, yes, *you* reading these words right now, are one with the All, the Everything, the entire Cosmos that predates even the big bang, in every waking second of your life.

Ultimate truth is infinite and completely free from all finite qualities or characteristics. It's formless and timeless, having no space and never changing. The relative world and its manifestations are but ornaments of this ever-present everything that is the ground of all being, of all forms.

In Buddhism, the ultimate or absolute truth is called *dharmakaya,* which, while recognized as the formless, ultimate nature of all things, still has an aspect of cognizance, one that incorporates all material things and is the ground of their manifestation. As Vajrayana master, scholar, poet, and head of the Nyingma school of Tibetan Buddhism Dilgo Khyentse teaches in *The Hundred Verses of Advice,* "The dharmakaya, the absolute dimension, the ultimate nature of everything, is emptiness. . . . It has a cognitive, radiant clarity aspect that knows all phenomena and manifests spontaneously. The dharmakaya is not something produced by causes and conditions; it is the primordially present nature of the mind."[2]

As we see from Dilgo Khyentse's words, this ultimate truth of dharmakaya is the ever-present nature of mind and is beyond the effect of any cause or condition. It simply is as it is. Dharmakaya is only one third of the Buddhist Trikāya doctrine (three bodies or three aspects of personality), however. There is also the relative, or form body, that is known as *nirmanakaya,* an example of which would be Shakyamuni Buddha, who took birth to teach and liberate others. Then there's *sambhogakaya,* which is the body that brings together the absolute (dharmakaya) with the relative (nirmanakaya), in a way that the relative body experiences the bliss of realizing the absolute.

That's just a Buddhist example, one that not even all schools of Buddhism would necessarily agree on (which is fine because, remember, it's all about honoring our own truth). In Christian mysticism, the absolute is often referred to as the Godhead; in Hinduism, it's Brahman; in Taoism, it's the Tao, and on and on the examples go. What all of them share is the core teaching that there is a *source,* a place of complete nonduality from which all things rise. This place is one to which we're always connected. It's our own original, perfect, infinite, and boundless state.

Okay, so which is it? Are we that, or aren't we? Well, you're gonna hate me, but it's actually both . . . and it's neither, and I'm sorry, but I'm actually laughing a bit at the absurdity, the madness of all this as I sit here typing away. Yet, as I laugh, I honor that it's the crazy-ass truth that I've come to experience in my heart as the absolute realest of real experiences.

Who we really *are,* the formless, Witnessing Awareness, is never born and never dies. And we're able to have that experience of this Self, our truest Self, in this lifetime. For most people, it takes time, practice, compassion, and patience—lots and lots of patience—to get to this place, though in reality, it's already right here, right now, within us as Everything Mind.

So let's take a nice, deep breath now—I imagine some of you are a bit frazzled at this point. (I know I am.) Much of this material seemed nonsensical to me at first, and occasionally, some of it still does, but isn't life pretty nonsensical? If we take an honest look at life for what it really is, most of us would agree that it's an epically strange experience.

Maybe the mystics, saints, yogis, and scholars who came before us really were onto something with their crazy wisdom teachings: fighting fire with fire, which is to say, meeting this fluid and strange human existence with fluid and strange teachings.

I know all too well that processing some of this material can be tricky. It's not always easy to dig deep and open our minds to new ideas and concepts, especially the ones presented here. But as we continue exploring and working with them, they will create a true understanding and experience of peace, compassion, intuition, and overall greater well-being. We'll begin to experience life as no longer happening to us but, rather, through us, and there's so much freedom in that. These aren't empty promises. Please, try this stuff out and see for yourself!

I suspect that many of you reading these words already intuitively know, or more importantly *feel*, what's meant underneath the abstract teachings and strange implications I just shared with you. So all I ask of you now is to please sit with what you've just read, take it all to heart, and then, when you're ready, turn the page.

I'm just a pigeon with one mile left
That doggy-paddles through this
bullshit ocean of death.

CANNIBAL OX, "PIGEON"

PRACTICE

DIE, DIE, MY DARLING

One way to better understand our own being/not being is by experiencing our own deaths. (In practice, not literally of course.) This is a powerful tool for loosening our identification with our bodies and senses. As we do so, we create a space to experience the nondual state of Spirit, God, Stillness, Buddha Mind, Cosmic Christ, Everything Mind, lessening our fears and anxieties around our inevitable death.

At the same time, practicing our own death can help us to deepen our appreciation for the "simpler" things in our lives—family and friends, the latest issue of *Thrasher* magazine, a sunrise or sunset, the smell of freshly cut grass, a good cup of coffee, an episode of *Twin Peaks*. We can enjoy it all from a place of greater reverence, with the respect and knowledge that nothing on the material level will last forever.

Please, please, please, understand that I am not saying that death *is* the answer! Absolutely no way. In fact, this practice may not be suited for those struggling with depression issues. I would never want it to be misunderstood as a glamorization of death, or something that leads someone to believe that death in and of itself is in any way the answer. *It is not.* If you're reading this while you're struggling with depression, yet haven't talked to someone on a professional level about it (a doctor, psychiatrist, or counselor), please do so, and do so as soon as possible. I speak from firsthand experience that life can, and does, get better, and there is absolutely no need for you to have to live from a place of sadness or hopelessness on a consistent basis. Sometimes we just need a bit of outside help.

With that said, the following practice is my own interpretation of a death meditation taught by Laura Huxley (wife of the brilliant Aldous Huxley). I've found it to be extremely beneficial not only in helping me unravel much of my fear surrounding death (though I'd be lying if I said there still wasn't some fear hanging on in there—practice and not perfection, though, right?) but also in experiencing the nondual state of Everything Mind. So here goes:

- In a darkened room, lie down and get comfortable. Begin by letting go of your body, imagining that you're dead. Imagine that your body is lifeless and, having served its purpose this time around, is no longer "yours."

- Explore this empty and alone sensation of no longer having a body, letting the experience take you wherever it goes—even if this results in screaming, crying, and swearing. No matter how uncomfortable or awkward it may get, just stay with it.

- When you feel like you've truly connected with the experience of letting your body go, imagine yourself at your funeral, your last grand hoorah! Take time to talk to friends and family who are in attendance. Tell them everything you ever wanted to but, for whatever reason, felt as though you couldn't before dying. Tell them all your fears, mistakes, suffering, embarrassments, and joys. Let it all out because you no longer have to fear what anyone else thinks. This is your final good-bye, so don't hold anything back.

- After saying everything you've felt moved to, make your way over to the casket. Look at your corpse. Allow whatever emotions come up to come up. If you find yourself crying, go ahead and cry . . . cry until there are no more tears left. Allow all the pain, resentment, bitterness, fear, hurt, and sadness buried within your heart to flow out with every tear.

- When you're ready, take the lifeless hand in the casket, raise it to your lips, and with love and reverence, kiss it, saying good-bye. Once you've said good-bye, allow the entire room to disappear so all that's left is your sense of I AMness.

- Stay in this place of I AMness for as long as feels right for you, and when you feel ready, gently bring yourself out of this visualization and back to your living body. Cultivate a feeling of loving freedom within yourself, and then allow it to spread from your heart to every single part of you—atoms, molecules, cells, bones, muscle, skin, and tissue—so that

it embodies your entire sense of being. As you move
forward in your waking life, continue cultivating this
feeling of love, respect, and gratitude in every moment,
allowing it to emanate through you and into the world
for all beings to enjoy.

For some, this practice may be difficult at first. I know when I
began working with it, I experienced particular anxiety during
the "letting go of my body" part. Our ego hates that shit because
all it has is identification with our thoughts and physical being.
Yet as we anchor into the place of no body and reach that of
Witnessing Awareness (I AMness), the experience becomes
much more natural (even if we do find ourselves screaming
or crying).

When it comes to death and our fear around it, the Indian
philosopher Krishnamurti once said, "We separate death as
something horrible, something to be frightened about. And to
us, this living, which is misery, we accept. If we didn't accept this
existence as misery, then life and death are the same movement.
Like love, death and living are one."[1] Or in the words of Kahlil
Gibran, "For what is it to die but to stand naked in the wind
and to melt into the sun?"[2] There truly isn't anything to fear in
death, and if we become more intimate with it *now*, rather than
later when its presence is upon us, our transition will be one of
peace, grace, and ease—as will our life in the meantime.

Imitation gets you so far,
but it kills from within.

UNBROKEN, "D4"

NO APOLOGIES

ne of the beneficial side effects of working with the death meditation practice (and the other practices in this book) is that it will make clear that spending time worrying what other people think about your spiritual practice or who you are as an individual in general is a complete waste of time. It's okay to be yourself on the spiritual path, to look inside and honor *your* truth, because whatever resonates as true for you is all-good in Everything Mind (while staying open to change and continued growth). You don't need to start dressing a certain way or using certain words or listening to certain types of music.

Yes, you are bound to run into people who will give you a hard time because you don't fit the mold of what they believe spirituality is supposed to look or sound like. But their opinions and judgments are on them, not you. Don't waste your time or energy feeding into close-mindedness. You're the only one who's going to know what *your* truth is, which, as we covered earlier, can be done by tuning into your heart center. So go with that! Look inside; become as intimate with your discerning heart as you possibly can, because that is the greatest friend and guide you'll have on the spiritual journey.

It's certainly true that the words of those who've walked the path before us are a huge help in guiding our way. Words and teachings are important for facilitating our awakening, but it's the *experiences* we have that bring the words and teachings to life. And those experiences can never be found in the words, or even the teachings themselves. Words and teachings are nothing more than symbols—they show us the way, but they are not the way. We're the ones who have to do the legwork. We have to find and dedicate ourselves to the practices (both traditional and nontraditional) that resonate for us, because the application of practice results in experience. Experience is the place where everything begins to change. But let's not forget that even the experiences themselves are just that: experiences—temporary glimpses into the purely nondualistic state of nonreturn that we're all bound to get to. It may happen in this lifetime, or it may happen in another, but inevitably, it's going to happen. So seriously, it's in your best interest to take it easy on yourself as you go about this spirituality business.

Now, how will we know for sure we're on the right path? How will we know we're making the right amount of progress in the right amount of time? The truth is, we're usually not going to know. If we cultivate a sincere trust in the process, take guidance from those we respect (both alive *and* dead), and again, most importantly, tune into our hearts for sincere guidance, we're well on our way.

I was recently teaching an online class called "Finding Your Own Spiritual Path" with my friends Adam Bucko (coauthor of the wonderful book *Occupy Spirituality*) and Andrew Harvey (whom I've already talked about). Andrew addressed two very important pitfalls we should all be aware of when setting out on a path of direct connection. The first is about listening to our heart's guidance, and Andrew said:

> It is often very difficult to tell the difference between the authentic guidance of the heart and your own confused desires to seeing something or other happen in a certain situation. So unless you develop deep discernment and have some inner experience of the difference between the you that is driven by karma, driven by ego, and the you that arises in spaciousness and love when you are freed from karma and ego, it's going to be hard to really hear what your true voice is saying.[1]

What Andrew is saying is that we need to really check our motives and be completely honest with ourselves on the spiritual path. Are we hearing only what we *want to hear* from our hearts, or are we listening with a truly open and discerning mind? Only you can know for sure, but you have to be brutally honest with yourself.

The second pitfall Andrew addressed is becoming narcissistic in our practice: worrying only about ourselves and focusing only on things like how much progress we're making on our path or how many sutras we've memorized or how many mantras we've said in a day. Of course, those things can be important, but there's also a shitload of work to be done in the world; and you, in countless ways, are able to contribute to the betterment of humanity and make a sincere difference. Andrew elaborated by saying:

> When you are listening to your heart to find out what your true path is, don't just listen to your own heart as

it refers to your own life: "Are you lonely? Do you long for a lover? Is your primal connection with God through passionate love with reality?" Don't just listen in that way; listen to your broken heart about the world. Listen to your broken heart about the holocaust of the animals, about the destruction of the environment, about the tragic way in which poor people are kept by a system that thrives on poverty. Listen to your heart about racism, when you're seeing again and again that video of the beautiful, Shambhalic black man being killed by cops [Eric Garner]. Listen to your heart, because your heart will tell you that it is not enough to have a spiritual path that pursues your own private liberation; you must pursue a path that frees you and liberates you in order for you to turn out more passionately, more steadily, more groundedly in the real world to be an agent, an instrument, of God's will for transformation of this world into being a living mirror of God's love and justice.[2]

So find out what *your* truth is and own that shit, but own it with an open heart, an open mind, and in a way that benefits others in the process. Finding the balance can be tricky and may take some time, so just do your best and be gentle with yourself in the process.

It's also worth mentioning that what resonates as truth for you one day may not the next, and that's okay too. Gandhi once said, "I am human, and I make mistakes. Therefore my commitment must be to truth and not to consistency."[3] This is a perfect place to experience life from, because who knows what tomorrow's experience of truth will bring for you or for any of us. As we keep our hearts and minds open in this way, we're open to life and its deeper meanings.

Cracks in the ceiling,
crooked pictures in the heart.

QUEENS OF THE STONE AGE, "IN THE FADE"

TONY HAWK, PUBLIC ENEMY, AND THE UNIVERSE INSIDE

Sometimes I feel trapped in the relative level—bound to this physical body and material universe. It's an intimate—and at times horribly claustrophobic—feeling, this trapped-ness. I spent many years somewhat baffled by it because I'm fine in tight situations, like a crammed elevator. Hell, I'm even good to go in show and concert environments—from small punk clubs filled with sweaty, adrenalized people going nuts, to larger hip-hop festivals, I don't feel the slightest tinge of anxiety or claustrophobia. Still, on occasion, and in times of solitude, I feel as though I'm a prisoner in my own skin, bones, muscle, and veins.

Throughout the years, these self-contracting and chest-tightening experiences, besides being a serious pain in my ass, have become a blessing in disguise. I say that because they inspired me to deepen my meditation practice, which time and again has left me with the experience and awareness that I am much more than *just* this physical body even though I may at times feel bound by it.

Before I go any further, it's important to note that shunning our physical bodies as burdens on our spiritual journey is not only futile, but also a great waste of time. Christ, just look at the Buddha who spent all those years as an ascetic, trying all sorts of practices that brought him to the brink of death, only to find liberation on the *middle path* (cultivating a practice somewhere *between* indulgence in pleasures and inviting self-harm).

With time spent sincerely in meditation and other practices, we can experience the transcendence of our thoughts, emotions, and physical bodies as we delve into our Everything Minds and deepen our familiarity with the Witnessing Awareness of all that is arising (which also includes our physical bodies). And as I mentioned earlier, this Witness is actually right here, right now, already coexisting with our normal waking consciousness.

So then, what's stopping us from experiencing this Witness on a regular and consistent basis? Well, we're conscious beings who, for the most part, experience said consciousness smack-dab in the middle of our heads. It's as if there were a small being navigating our lives from a captain's chair in the middle of our skull—which results in our identification with our physical bodies, thoughts, and emotions as the ultimate truth of who we are.

For example, right now, from my ego's perspective, I, Chris Grosso, am experiencing my physical body sitting in a slightly chilly room, listening to Deafheaven and trying to think of witty and accessible ways to explain this rather daunting topic. The room I'm sitting in is in a house, which is surrounded by grass, trees, birds, and all sorts of other nature-y goodness; and all that is surrounded by the sky—a sky that extends out into the farthest reaches of the universe.

From my ego's perspective, this is a completely accurate depiction of my immediate reality. And while many of the great wisdom traditions assert that yes, our physical bodies are of course a part of the equation, they're also very clear that they're not the be-all and end-all we think they are. And this is where ultimate reality comes in, and concepts such as dharmakaya, Spirit, God, and Brahman are meditated upon.

Now this Spirit (or whatever you choose to call It) is a pretty amazing thing. So amazing, in fact, that Zen masters have said It can swallow the entire Pacific Ocean in one gulp. . . . One gulp! At face value this whole "one gulp" thing might sound a bit ridiculous, and that's fair. When we explore the implications (through things like meditation, mantra, yoga) of who we are *beyond* our finite physical selves, if we stick with it long enough, we'll inevitably start having some experiences that result in that "one gulp" statement making sense. (Remember that it's only through personal experience that things like this go from sounding completely bat-shit crazy to making sense.)

I'll try to explain this insane-sounding—yet completely-natural-once-experienced—statement. Here goes: The reason we, as Spirit, can drink the entire Pacific Ocean in one gulp is because, when the strict identification with ourselves as bodies and senses is set aside, no matter how temporarily, we come to see—better yet, come to *know*—that we *are* the entire Pacific Ocean. More specifically, in this place, we embody Witnessing Awareness, which as we've established, underlies our entire physical, manifest experience.

Anyway, returning to my initial example of the whole room/house/nature/listening to Deafheaven thing (and by the way, their *Sunbather* album is incredible and you should buy it, though by the time this book is out, they'll probably have a new album, which I'm sure will be equally as good, so you should probably buy that, too), let's revisit it from the place of Witnessing Awareness rather than ego.

As the Witness, I gaze across this room and still "see" everything as I normally would—noticing things like musical instruments scattered here and there, a wall decorated with various prints from Public Enemy to Ram Dass, some Star Wars action figures on a shelf, and my very first Tony Hawk skateboard in the corner. And as I rest in this Witnessing Awareness (rather than my ego self), I experience, in crystal clarity, that neither my body nor any of these *things* are actually out there, or even in the universe at all. Instead, my body and these things (which even include the universe itself) are *all* within Me—within the Witnessing Awareness that at my core, and at your core, We truly are.

In this recognition, there is no room left for any of the claustrophobic feelings of trapped-ness I'd previously felt, because I no longer identify with my body. In fact, I'm now free to experience this body as housed within Witnessing Awareness. It's in this place of Witnessing Awareness that swallowing the entire Pacific Ocean in a single gulp makes more sense than anything else I know. *This* is the place of Everything Mind, where the relative truth of form and the absolute truth of formlessness are equally embraced and experienced. *Huzzah!*

The only way to find true happiness
is to risk being completely cut open.

CHUCK PALAHNIUK

23

ON SUFFERING
(And How to Fit the Entire Human Race into a Single Sugar Cube)

As I was writing the preceding chapter and glanced over at my old Tony Hawk skateboard, it brought back some memories that reminded me of how, for the greater part of my teenage and early adult years, I felt like I deserved to suffer. Since then, I've become enthralled with trying to better understand suffering and its root causes. My exploration and studies led me to a quote from spiritual teacher Ram Dass, who wrote, "Suffering is the sandpaper of our incarnation. It does its work of shaping us."[1]

While at first glance this statement may sound rather simple, as I took it deeper into my heart and spent time truly contemplating what it meant, I found myself becoming profoundly affected by it. That simple statement helped me realize that, even though I had yet to understand much of the rationale behind both my mental and emotional turmoil—*and* the subsequent unskillful ways in which I lived to avoid feeling and working through said turmoil—at the very least, all my past suffering wasn't for nothing.

I also realized that I could use the mental and physical discomfort I residually experience as a transformational tool. Instead of becoming comfortably numb by ingesting various substances, I face my past and all its fucked-up wreckage. I completely open my heart to the pain of those dark times while I explore my uncomfortable thoughts, emotions, and memories when they arise; and through these modest acts of bravery, I am able to begin transmuting the pain, the heartache, and the misery into compassion for both others and myself. What's done is done. We can't change the past, but we can make amends by doing our best to be better people each day, offering our lives and those in it our best possible selves.

Another thing I began to recognize while sitting with Ram Dass's words was that, on a broader scale, much of the suffering that is rampant in people's lives today goes unnoticed by them. This might sound weird to some of you, because it would seem that if we're in pain or we're suffering, then we'd know it and do something about it, right? Well, this is partially correct. Larger-scale pain and suffering, like the loss of a loved one or pain surrounding any other kind of traumatic event, is virtually impossible to ignore, so we each consciously deal with it in our own ways (healthy or not). It's the lower levels of pain and suffering that usually go unnoticed—that's because we're used to them. For example, feelings of discontentment with our job, our love life, our home, or our physical appearance are just a few things that cause many of us to experience an underlying shitty feeling throughout our days . . . and usually without our even knowing it.

One of the Buddha's primary teachings is the Four Noble Truths. These are:

1. Human existence is characterized by suffering. (Some Buddhist teachers note that "suffering" was taken out of context, or mistranslated from the Buddha's original teachings, and instead should be replaced with the word "unsatisfactory." Either way, you get the point.)

2. There are causes for our suffering and unsatisfactory experiences in life, which include craving, aversion, desire, attachment, and ignorance.

3. Freedom from this suffering is possible.

4. There is a path to freedom, known as the Eightfold Path, which consists of right understanding, right intention, right speech, right action, right livelihood, right effort, right mindfulness, and right concentration.

If we really think about the Buddha's first two Noble Truths in the context of our lives, we can see that, yes, in birth there is suffering (or unsatisfactory-ness), in aging there is suffering, in sickness there is suffering, in not getting what we want there is suffering. Hell, even in getting what we want there can be suffering if we attach or cling to it for a sense of peace and happiness.

The good news is that there's grace to be found in this suffering if we can open our heart to it and work with the pain—whether using the Eightfold Path or other means that feel right for us (like the Unconditional Love and Acceptance practice on page

115, or the Shadow Self practice on page 71). If we work with the pain from a place of Witnessing Awareness rather than the ego, which will want to turn away from it in fear, we begin to see that our pain and its various forms of discomfort are simply byproducts of our human experience. This is not to diminish them or say that we won't still feel them, but the experience will become significantly less personal.

When we no longer identify ourselves as the unpleasant emotions, spaciousness opens up around our uncomfortable experiences; it's a liberating, subtle shift and it happens when we're rooted in the Witnessing Awareness. Over time, from this place of Witnessing Awareness, it becomes increasingly clear that we are so much more than just our thoughts, emotions, and physical bodies—which, when we're attached to them as our ultimate reality, are the root of our suffering.

Now, here's a random fun fact: we are made of atoms, which are 99.99999 percent empty space. So basically, if you were to squeeze the space out of all the atoms of all the people in the world, the entire human race would fit into a sugar cube.[2] You may be thinking, "Interesting, but what am I supposed to do with that information?" Well, my point isn't so much about the information itself but rather its implications: that many of us have been living with our head in the sand, from believing that our ingrained perception of reality is the only reality to believing that living with all the aforementioned suffering is actually necessary.

I'm trying to offer a gentle wake-up call here to those of us who have become indifferent in life, accepting this underlying stress, pain, and suffering simply because it's what we've come to know as familiar, and believing familiarity is safe. Sometimes familiarity *is* safe, but not when it leads to an unnecessary lack of well-being. For me, suffering has now become a reminder, an invitation to remember that I am much more than this physical body, the 99.99999 percent empty space I've strictly identified with for so many years. With that remembering comes a lot of peace.

Of course, on the relative level, we are our physical selves, but the *awareness* of our physical selves (which is beyond the limits of our rational, thinking mind) offers us the possibility to experience life without taking things so personally. The dumb shit we did in our younger years, or hell, that we may have done last week, no longer needs to be a source of our suffering. We learn from our mistakes and make amends both with ourselves and—wherever and whenever possible—with those we may have harmed. Then we let it go; we move on. The greatest gift we can offer others and ourselves as we're cultivating a deeper experience of Everything Mind is our own being, so why not make that the best possible being we can?

There is no reality except the one contained within us. That is why so many people live such an unreal life. They take the images outside of them for reality and never allow the world within to assert itself.

HERMAN HESSE

PRACTICE

ONE WITH THE ETERNAL EVERYTHING
(Guided Meditation)

While I'm not huge on guided meditations, the following is an abridged version of one I learned from Ram Dass's wonderful book *Polishing the Mirror*,[1] and that I incorporate into my practice from time to time. It's a wonderful way of experiencing the unfolding evolution of Spirit as well as cultivating the experience of our Witnessing Awareness, not to mention Everything Mind. Here's an abridged breakdown, bullet-point style for you:

• Begin by closing your eyes and, as with any type of meditation practice, sit as straight as you can without being overly rigid. Just make sure your spine is erect, your shoulders and belly relaxed, your chin slightly tucked in so your neck is in alignment with your spine, and from there you're good to go. Once you've found your sweet spot, proceed to take three deep in- and out-breaths, either through your nose or mouth. (Whichever feels right for you is totally cool.)

- Bring your awareness to your heart center (located in the middle of your chest) and once there, begin to breathe. This no ordinary breathing you're going to be doing, though. Nope, instead imagine that your heart is doing the breathing—in and out of your chest—rather than in and out of your nose or mouth. This may seem weird to some people at first, which is totally fine; just stick with it for a moment or two, and you'll feel more comfortable and anchored into it.

- Once this heart breathing feels natural, imagine yourself surrounded by illumined teachers that inspire you on your spiritual path. Maybe there's the Buddha or Christ or Krishna; possibly Black Elk, Gandhi, Anandamayi Ma, Krishnamurti, Teresa of Ávila, Ramana Maharshi, the Virgin Mary, Ramakrishna, Maharajji, or Paramahansa Yogananda; or maybe none of these, which is absolutely fine. The important thing is to imagine whoever is an inspiration for *your* spiritual journey.

- As these illumined beings surround you, picture a golden mist leaving their bodies and filling the air. With each breath you take in (still breathing from your heart center), breathe this golden mist into you, all the way down to the tips of your toes, and all the way back up to the top of your head. Breathe it in until your entire body is full of this golden mist, and then, on each out-breath, release any negative feelings you become aware of. Take a moment to see if you've been suppressing (consciously or otherwise) any unpleasant thoughts or emotions. They may be subtle, so be sure to really give yourself a few moments to allow anything unpleasant to make itself known to you, and after it does, release it by breathing it out.

- Now, bring your focus back to your heart center, and as you do, draw all the golden mist that's inside of you, from your head to your toes, into the middle of your chest. This is another part of the meditation that may be a little weird for some people, but I encourage you to lay aside whatever thoughts your mind may be conjuring and just roll with it. This meditation is worth it in the end—I promise! So imagine the golden mist you've just drawn into your heart center taking the shape of a tiny being (roughly the size of your thumb) and sitting on top of a lotus blossom.

- Picture this tiny being sitting peacefully, emanating a quiet radiance throughout your heart center with light shining in every possible direction from his/her/its essence. This being represents the embodiment of complete and perfect wisdom, compassion, and love. Allow yourself to feel these qualities arising in you as much as possible. If for any reason you're having trouble feeling these qualities, remind yourself that they are all a part of your inherent, natural state, and, regardless of whether you've been on the spiritual path for one day, or fifty years, it's your right to experience and embody them.

- Now, visualize this tiny being expanding until he/she/it fills your entire body—from the top of your head, down through your chest and stomach, into your arms, legs, fingers, and toes. Recognize your communion with this being as *yourself.* Feel its perfect love, joy, and compassion.

- When you feel ready, slowly let this being—who you now are rather than your physical body—grow in size so that it encompasses within itself everything in your immediate surroundings. Everything you're aware of, the sights, sounds, and even the physical body you normally identify with, is now inside of you as *this being.*

- Continue to grow in size until your head reaches the sky. Look down and see that things like your local coffee shop, skate park, library, yoga studio, family, friends, and strangers passing by are all within you. Look down with great compassion on all this, acknowledging the myriad human experiences that are happening—the suffering and love, the hope and hopelessness—because all this too is within you.

- Continue growing in size until you're in the middle of the galaxy. The earth is now deep within your belly, and all humanity is within you—as are all its pleasures and pains. Feel them deeply and, in your perfect peace and compassion, extend all beings love.

- When you feel ready, grow even larger, expanding so that every galaxy and all creation is within you.

Feel your ISness, your perfect peace. Become aware of your boundlessness. There is no one else but you—time immemorial and even beyond that is who you are. As you rest in this place of stillness, notice that even the awareness of all the galaxies is beginning to fade as you dissolve into complete abstraction, a perfect nondual formlessness.

- Honor this place of complete perfection for as long as feels right, and when you're ready, slowly begin taking form again. Come back from the farthest reaches of the galaxy until you're looking down again upon the earth.

- Continue returning slowly, until your head is back at the top of the room where you began this meditation. Once there, look down and see your material self seated in meditation. Recognize the fears, doubts, and anything else that your physical body may be clinging to, and then look beyond those feelings and remember the purity of who you really are.

- As your still-large and illumined Self, reach down, gently placing your hand (metaphorically of course) on your meditating self's head. Extend the perfect love and compassion that you are to your physical self so that it too may come to know and experience the truth of who you really are.

- When you're ready, re-enter your body and stay there for a moment, completely engulfed in the perfect light, love, compassion, and joy that you are as this being. While there, extend these feelings of love and compassion to all beings, everywhere. Send these loving feelings to those who are healthy and those who are sick, those in your community and those on the other side of the planet. *All beings, everywhere, send them all love.*

- Now, watch this being continue to shrink in size (again, to roughly that of a thumb) in your heart center and return to the top of the lotus blossom. The being continues to radiate light, love, compassion, and well-being. This tiny form of the entire universe knows all and is all within you. All you need to do is simply quiet your mind to connect with him/her/it, because in the depths of reality, this being is the truth of who you really are. As you go about your days, please take time to remember yourself as such, sharing your brilliant love and compassion with this weird and beautiful and scary and inspiring world.

It's a trap!

ADMIRAL ACKBAR, IN *STAR WARS,*
EPISODE VI: THE RETURN OF THE JEDI

24

BLEED INTO ONE

The deeper we go with meditations such as the One with the Eternal Everything, the more we naturally and effortlessly begin to experience life from the place of Everything Mind. We strengthen our connection to the place of boundless Witnessing Awareness, which, as an added bonus, makes navigating life's difficulties easier, as we now experience them in a significantly less personal way. Imagine you're sitting on a small stage in a room with roughly a hundred people who have gathered to hear you give a talk on Buddhism. When you initially took the stage, you were, for the most part, relaxed. Then, just as you're about to begin the talk, your mind goes completely blank, not even knowing why you're on the stage in the first place.

You sit in a bewildered state as various forms of physical and mental anxiety begin to arise, when all of a sudden, something deep inside of you—below your conscious rational mind—begins to take over. This deeper wisdom guides you to close your eyes, place your palms together in front of your heart, and mindfully recite all the thoughts and emotions that are arising for you in the moment: "Afraid, embarrassed, confused, sense of dying, lost." After a few minutes of doing this, your body begins to relax, your mind calms, and your senses return. Slowly, you raise your head, look around the room, and begin to remember why you are there.

The preceding is actually a true story, though it's not mine. I read about "Jacob," an elderly man and longtime meditator who suffers from Alzheimer's disease, in Tara Brach's book *Radical Acceptance*.[1] His story reminded me of why I set out on a spiritual path in the first place: to cultivate greater equanimity in life no matter what comes my way, and to establish a deeper connection with God in the grand, nondual context of Everything Mind.

Having the addiction background that I do—which resulted in many of the shitty circumstances I've already covered—I was a poster boy for the hopeless. While Jacob's second nature was to turn inward and pay attention when shit hit the fan, mine was to get high. It didn't matter what the substance was; anything that kept me from having to face reality would do just fine. Unlike Jacob, during those years, I didn't have any spiritual reference to draw from, so I did what I had to in order to survive. If it hadn't been for the relief the drugs provided me, there's a good chance I'd be dead today. (The Catch-22 being that those drugs almost killed me numerous times as well. . . . Ah, life.)

Grace eventually entered my life in the form of a professor who turned me on to spirituality. And now, after years of cultivating an integral spiritual practice (including, among other things, meditation, prayer, exercise, and service work), more often than not, I'm able to navigate the difficult times in my life with that greater equanimity I initially set out looking for.

Life is still far from perfect. But now, when the shit hits the fan, I know there's nothing that any drug or sense-pleasing distraction can offer that one simple, conscious breath can't get me through. For it's in that one breath that the entire essence of our being—the perfect nondual Suchness from which all things arise—exists. And spiritual practice helps us live with the understanding that we're always just a moment away from a new breath, and with that, our already inherently perfect state of Divine Being. That is no small thing.

But there's also a trap that can come with our spiritual practice: becoming absorbed with our personal spiritual progress. (I know we briefly touched on this in chapter 21, but I believe it's important enough to quickly revisit, since self-absorption can really be a sneaky bastard.) It can start happening particularly once we begin to have exciting "peak" experiences that are a natural byproduct of things like meditation, prayer, and mantra. These peak experiences are alluring because the peace and liberation we experience as we're reconnecting with our ever-present Self through them is incredible. It then becomes tempting to continue seeking more peak experiences and the subsequent bliss, peace, and love they produce. Those qualities are important things to cultivate, but if that's all we're focusing on—the bliss of our own spiritual growth—and not caring about the external world, our practice has become narcissistic.

The Gospel according to John tells us that Jesus said, "I and the Father are one" (10:30), meaning that he recognized his true Divinity. This Divinity is within every one of us and all things manifest. How could it not be? The material world is that of Spirit continuing to awaken to more and more of Itself. According to many of the wisdom traditions, Spirit, on the level of form, began unfolding Itself at the big bang and will continue to unfold until all sentient beings have awakened, and then the entire process will start over again. (But in all fairness, who really knows for sure about that part?)

The Father (or Divine Mother, Brahman, Emptiness) and I *are* One. The same goes for you. We include all beings and all things. This is hidden in plain sight for us all to see. As we begin to experience this, let's please keep it in (Everything) mind so that our spiritual practices move forward with the intention of benefitting *all beings,* and not just ourselves. I hope that this sounds obvious, but, man, I've seen some things . . .

It is foolish to think that we will enter
heaven without entering into ourselves.

TERESA OF ÁVILA

PRACTICE

MARANATHA MANTRA

One teaching that helps me get in touch with the Divine that
contains all beings is something I've learned from a variety of
teachers over the years—*maranatha*. It is a powerful word that
appears at the end of Paul's First Letter to the Corinthians and
is also the final instruction of the book of Revelation ("Come,
Lord Jesus," [Rev. 22:20]. So the final teaching of the Bible is
maranatha, an Aramaic term that means "come Lord." (*Mar*
means "Lord"; *an*, "our"; and *atha*, "come.")

It is suggested that repetition of this mantra be done mentally and broken down into four parts, with each part, or sound,
coinciding with our in- and out-breath. For example, as we
inhale, we mentally recite "ma" and on the exhale "ra," then on
our next inhale "na" and on the exhale "tha" (the *h* is silent, so
this part is pronounced "ta"). As we repeat the mantra, it helps

to keep our awareness focused in our heart center because 1) keeping our attention anywhere internally helps calm our discursive mind, and 2) the entire experience of our life began in the heart center. Lest we forget, it was the first thing to develop while we were still in the womb, so what better place to go back to than the source itself, right?

Saying the mantra in sync with your breath and focusing on the heart center are only suggestions. As with anything, please tune in to your own internal guidance, and practice in accordance with that. Maybe it will lead you to place your focus on your third eye (the area between your eyebrows) rather than your heart center. Maybe, rather than following your breath and enunciating the mantra in sync with it, you'll be guided to use the mantra as a more cyclical repetition in your mind. Then again, maybe it will be none of these, and this mantra won't even resonate with you in the first place, and that's cool too.

I've found it to be one of the most powerful mantras I use when it comes to igniting my heart center with passion and commitment to spiritual practice, because, personally, I associate it with an image of Jesus, who holds a very dear and loving place in my heart. I'll go into greater detail about my love/hate relationship with Jesus in the next chapter, but for now I'll say that once I got over my angsty and misguided youthful hate, I've come to have a profound, deep love for Jesus. Therefore, I've found that invoking God (and Jesus) while doing this mantra helps me remember, and experience, my true Self, dissolving feelings of separation from others and from life, all while melting into the one true Spirit.

Regarding the Maranatha mantra, Andrew Harvey wrote:

When you say Maranatha, inwardly reflecting with the focused intensity of your entire being on the meaning of the sacred syllables "Our Lord, come" or "Come, O Lord," you will begin to see that they represent at once an invitation to Christ-consciousness to possess everything we are and transfigure it, and also an invitation of the Spirit of God to descend in a flame of charity upon the world and transform all existing conditions on earth. Maranatha is, then, a plea for personal transformation and for a transformation of the world into the Kingdom.[1]

This mantra, which aims to bring us to union with the Godhead, the Absolute, is not unlike repeating mantras from the world's other great traditions, whose goals are also often to reunite us with Source (regardless of what you choose to call it). If Christ isn't your thing, there are plenty of other options. For example, in the Hindu tradition there's "Sri Ram, Jai Ram, Jai, Jai, Ram" (which means "Beloved Ram, I honor You", and Ram can be likened to the beloved all-embracing Absolute); in the Buddhist tradition, "Om mani padme hum" ("I bow to the jewel in the lotus of the heart"); in the Muslim tradition, "Allahu akbar" ("God is great"); and in the Jewish tradition, "Shalom" ("Peace"). And of course, there's always the classic sacred sound of *om,* which is known as the sound of the universe.

As with everything else in this book and on your journey, find what works for you and go with that. It's all bringing us back home to Everything Mind anyway.

JESUS HATES ME?

 o about that love/hate relationship with Jesus I previously mentioned. You could say it all began in the early '90s during my teenage years, with my introduction to punk rock and hardcore music. Since then, I've been a proponent of the "question everything" mindset, which includes our thoughts, actions, motives, and of course, the spiritual teachers and teachings we encounter on the path. Not all spiritual teachers are going to resonate with everyone, and that's fine. But maybe it's worth taking a little time to explore why that is. Do we truly have a problem with the teacher and their teachings, or is our dislike based on an outdated paradigm?

To say I had a very negative view of Jesus when I was younger doesn't even begin to do it justice; I *hated* the idea of him. I even rocked a T-shirt that read, "Jesus Hates Me/So Fuck Him."

195

There was also the time when I was a senior in high school and I went on a field trip to a big college fair. There were some people standing outside who were, somewhat forcibly, handing Bibles to students as they walked in: so me being me at the time, I proceeded to take one of their Bibles and rip it up in front of them.

In all fairness, this *was* during my often misguided youth. In retrospect, I see that my overall disdain for Jesus had nothing to do with him or his teachings, but instead, everything to do with my frustration toward close-minded, fundamentalist Christians. I wasn't a fan of *any* fundamentalists, but growing up in the area where I did, Christianity was prominent, hence my lashing out at poor old JC.

Now the interesting thing is that a few years after all this, there was a period of time, albeit it a short one, when I found myself, um, kinda sorta into the Jesus of dogmatic churchianity. Yup, not too long after the "Jesus Hates Me/So Fuck Him" phase of my life, I found myself kneeling in front of the pulpit of a packed Pentecostal church in Holyoke, Massachusetts. I, one of only two white people among the hundreds in attendance, was accepting Jesus Christ as lord and savior into my life.

I'd just spent the last hour and a half listening to the church's preacher go nuts—running around, hollering, speaking in tongues, and so forth—while giving a sermon in Spanish, a language I don't even understand. For whatever reason, at the end of his fiery sermon, when he asked if anyone wanted to come up front and be prayed over, I felt compelled to go (which, again, was strange because I didn't understand a word that had been uttered).

So, how did I go from "Jesus Hates Me" to accepting him as my lord and savior? Well, it all happened while I was living in New Haven, Connecticut, where I was attending college, and it was also at the peak of my piercing phase. I had decided it was time to get my bridge pierced (top of the nose between the eyes), so I called my friend who was a professional piercer to schedule an appointment. (As a quick side note, if you're thinking about getting pierced, go to someone who really knows their craft! Otherwise, you truly run the risk of harming yourself.)

Something strange happened on that phone call to my friend. He told me he didn't pierce anymore because he'd given it up for Jesus. I laughed, saying something to the effect of, "Yeah, okay, so seriously, when can we make this happen?" to which he replied that he was serious, that he'd given up piercing. At that point, I knew he wasn't kidding. It caught me off guard because, like me, my friend had grown up in the punk/hardcore scene, and while there were a few Christian hardcore bands back then (there are many more these days, unlike the early to mid-90s), Christianity and organized religion in general weren't really a popular notion with most hardcore kids. (For the old-school hardcore kids reading this: yes, there were bands like Zao, 108, Cro-Mags, Shelter, Sons of Abraham, and so on that were rooted in various religions, but I think you'd have to agree that "religious" hardcore bands were, for the most part, rare.)

In that same phone call, my friend proceeded to tell me I should really go to church with him and his girlfriend to check it out. I politely said, "Um, yeah, sure, maybe sometime," knowing I had no intention of going. I caved shortly thereafter and agreed to take him up on his offer. I don't know why exactly. Maybe it was because I'd never actually been to church before, and I wanted to prove to myself that all my negative judgments and opinions were right. Maybe it was because I really liked my friend and felt like giving him the benefit of the doubt. Either way, about a week or so later, I met up with him, his girlfriend, and his girlfriend's mother, and we were on our way to church.

I already gave you a brief rundown of the service, and how, at the end of it, I went up front to be prayed over. So let's pick this back up right before that point, when I was still sitting in the pew. The whole thing was so strange. Honestly, I didn't know what the fuck I was doing sitting there. I hadn't planned to go to church with the outcome of me accepting Jesus into my life that day, or any other. It was just that, after the pastor asked if anyone wanted to come up front, I felt utterly compelled to go, but mentally wasn't willing to budge. The next thing I knew, it was as if a force outside of me made my body get up and go. Yeah, I know, that sounds all woo-woo and possibly like complete bullshit to some, but it's what happened. Hopefully by now you know I have zero reason to bother making any of this shit up.

When I was up front on my knees, a woman began praying over me. A minute or two into it, she asked if I wanted to accept Jesus into my life as my personal lord and savior. It was an interesting question, especially for someone who not only had never been to church before, but also wore a "Fuck Jesus" T-shirt. The strangest of the strange happened about a second after she asked me that question, when I heard myself blurt out, "Yes."

She read a verse from the Bible, and when she finished, she asked me to declare that I accepted Christ into my life as "my lord and savior," which I did. I can say with all sincerity that, once I finished uttering those words, I immediately experienced a significant shift, one of feeling lighter, from my head to my toes. This could have just been me totally feeding into the experience and projecting onto it whatever I thought it was supposed to feel like. I was eighteen at the time, but still, I remember it being a pretty undeniable feeling.

Over the course of the next year, my ex-piercer friend and I became much closer as we visited various churches across Connecticut and Massachusetts. I even went to a Christian camp with him for a week, along with a bunch of the people from the church in Holyoke. I really got into the Christian thing in that short period of time. I plastered my car with all sorts of stickers like "Jesus Died 4 Your Sins" and of course the quintessential silver fish. I also started listening to cheesy Christian music and watching low-budget and poorly acted Christian movies. (I'm not trying to sound like a judgmental prick about Christian entertainment. I know all religions have cheesy music and poorly acted films, but these are just the ones I'm familiar with.)

At one point, I was so enthralled by my Christian experience that I renounced all secular music and destroyed all my non-Christian CDs, demo tapes, and records. (There was some really good rare stuff in that collection, especially the vinyl—bands like Sick of It All, Youth of Today, Deadguy, Inside Out, Quicksand, Converge, Snapcase, Cable). I didn't stop there—I snuck into my younger brother's room and destroyed his collection of CDs, demos, and vinyl, too! Yup, total dick-brother lifetime achievement award right there. (To be matched only by the time I missed his wedding, where I was supposed to be best man, because I was in detox. And yet, we're still super close. How lucky am I?) No matter how deep into the Christian thing I got, what never sat right with me was how the majority of the churches and churchgoers I encountered believed in the "our way is the only right way" teachings, along with the "everyone else is going to burn in hell" and "homosexuality is a sin" bullshit.

I may appear to be shining a negative light on Christianity, so it's important to note that in the twenty years since my experience with it, I've seen a tremendous shift in many churches' and Christians' attitudes—especially regarding the acceptance of others' religions and personal lifestyle choices, which is awesome. In no way do I mean to sit here and say Christianity is awful. After all, I'm just sharing with you my short-lived observation of the formal church aspect of it, which again, was some twenty years ago. I'm sure someone living in the Far East could write a similarly disenfranchised piece about their experience with whatever religious tradition is prevalent there. So there's that.

Since that time, I've met and been blessed to work with many inspiring Christians—people who truly embody the love and compassion that Christ taught. I also have a lot of really great friends who call themselves Christians, people who, I believe, exemplify the true heart of Jesus and his teachings beyond my own limited experience of churchianity and its drawbacks. Hell, some of the practices in this book are drawn from the Christian tradition, so hopefully it's clear that I honor the heart of Christianity and all its wonderful contemplatives and mystics.

I don't recall what specifically made me stop going to church, or reading my Bible, or why I said good-bye to the corny movies and music. I'm sure part of it was because I felt tied down to beliefs that didn't resonate in my heart, and certainly part of it was because I was young with a rebellious heart: feeling like there was still a lot of shit I had left to fuck up.

The one thing that's never left me is that experience of the presence of Christ. As much as I absolutely love and honor the great wisdom traditions of the East, I've always felt drawn toward Christ's presence the most. It's as if Jesus has been hanging out in my heart since then and whispering to me, "Okay, how can we use this rebellious heart of yours to wake your ass up . . . and while we're at it, be of service to others?"

I have a lot of love for that longhaired, love-preaching mystic. I believe he's guided me through some seriously heavy shit in my life, which has inevitably led not only to the fact that I'm still alive, but able to be of service. I'm also able to live from a place where I'm comfortable enough to talk about Jesus, even if it may not seem cool. I have no problem saying how extremely important his presence is in my life, while still honoring all my other great teachers: Maharajji, punk rock and hardcore,

Buddha, hip-hop, Kali, skateboarding, addiction, recovery, friends and family.

Jesus was an illumined teacher in exactly the same way the Buddha, Krishna, Lao Tsu, Ramana Maharshi, Ramakrishna, and many others were. He's gotten a really bad rap from a lot of people here in the West due to overzealous fundamentalists preaching half-truths (if even that), and politicians twisting the Bible to fit whatever bullshit agenda they're trying to push. Again, the same could be said for virtually all religions that inevitably have their share of fundamentalist followers.

I'm so glad I was able to call bullshit on myself and cultivate a tremendously beautiful relationship with Jesus (along with many other illumined teachers) and to not be ashamed or embarrassed to talk about it. I'm not saying I'm going to wear a "Jesus Is My Homeboy" T-shirt or watch Kirk Cameron movies, but the real-deal Jesus is right on in my book. I'm sincerely grateful to him for being a huge catalyst in my experience of Everything Mind, and I honor him as one of the great teachers in my life.

I was never really insane except upon
occasions when my heart was touched.

EDGAR ALLAN POE

PRACTICE

CENTERING PRAYER

Besides the presence of Jesus, another element of Christianity I've taken into my heart is centering prayer. Based on *The
Cloud of the Unknowing,* an anonymous text of Christian mysticism from the fourteenth century, the core of its emphasis is
that Christ, in this and every moment, is alive within us as the
Enlightened One. This Enlightened One has little to do with
the physical manifestation of a person or deity and instead is
much more about the state of perfect ISness, or I AMness, that
is beyond all form and name within Everything Mind.

Centering prayer is a way of opening ourselves to God's presence in our lives. Prayer is traditionally thought of as bringing
our hopes, dreams, fears, and worries to God, but centering
prayer varies in that it is a receptive form of prayer. It helps us

anchor into a calm stillness, allowing us to experience God's already-existent presence within us.

The interesting thing about centering prayer is that the actual results usually don't happen while we're praying. Instead, these practices help us to center our hearts and minds in a place of alert readiness to feel God's presence—anytime, anywhere. And when I say anywhere, I mean *anywhere:* from hardcore and hip-hop shows to drive-in movie theaters and yoga classes; while reading a book, taking an exam, shopping at a record store . . . anywhere means anywhere!

It is recommended that this practice be done twice a day (once in the morning and once in the afternoon or evening) for roughly twenty minutes each time. As we go deeper into centering prayer, our relationship with Christ shifts from that of mere acquaintance to one of actual friendship, trust, and love. It's through this experience that we learn to rest in God as the perfect stillness that we truly are. As Father Thomas Keating, who revived the practice in the 1970s along with Father William Meninger and Dom M. Basil Pennington, has said about it, "We open our awareness to God whom we know by faith is within us, closer than breathing, closer than thinking, closer than choosing—closer than consciousness itself."[1]

The practice is relatively simple and can be broken down into the following four steps, which I learned from the teachings of Father Thomas Keating:[2]

1. Choose any sacred word that resonates with you as a symbol of God, doing so with the understanding that you consent to God's presence and action within you. There's a recommendation to ask the Holy Spirit for guidance in choosing this word, but I leave that entirely up to your discretion. Some examples of

sacred words are: Jesus, Mary, Mother, Father, Jesu, Abba, Mater. But you may also be guided to a more general word such as: love, stillness, shalom, peace, or amen. Once you have your word, use it for the duration of your time spent in centering prayer. You may feel tempted to cover more than one base by incorporating a few different words, but this keeps our thinking minds activated during the prayer. We want to allow our mind to come to a point of stillness, which happens as we calm down through the repetition of a single word.

2. Find a comfortable sitting position. If you've spent any time in meditation, you already know the drill, but just in case you haven't, be sure that your spine is erect while you relax your shoulders and belly. Keep your neck elongated yet relaxed, tucking your chin in slightly toward your chest. Imagine the crown of your head being drawn upward, as if a puppeteer were pulling it up by a string. Once you've found your sweet spot, close your eyes and take a moment to settle into silence. When you're ready, gently introduce your sacred word inwardly, which represents the symbolic gesture of your consent to God's presence and action within you.

3. If, or I should really say when, you become aware that you're lost in thought (it's pretty much inevitable that this will happen and is completely normal), gently and effortlessly bring your attention back to your sacred word. Some people have a tendency to beat themselves up when their thoughts

wander during meditation, as if they were failing at their practice. Well, here's some friendly advice that I wish I had taken to heart when I first began meditating: *do not be one of those people!* Seriously, we've been lost in thought for the greater part of our lives, so for most of us, it takes awhile to change this. Through dedicated practice, we naturally become more centered with the Witnessing Awareness that underlies the thoughts as they come and go, and when we reach this place, we'll be less swayed by our discursive minds.

4. When you finish approximately twenty minutes in prayer, allow yourself a few moments to slowly reorient back into your normal waking consciousness, even if you find your experience didn't go very "deep" while you were praying. What I mean by "deep" is that, through the cyclic repetition of our sacred word, our consciousness will often slowly sink back into itself. When this happens, our experience becomes one of Being, where even the awareness of our bodies falls away as we reside in a simple state of ISness. If this happens, great, but if it doesn't happen, that's totally cool too. The fact that you're dedicating yourself to such a profound practice not only for your betterment but also for all beings is huge in and of itself. So seriously, take pride in that. For whatever it's worth, I have much love and respect for you doing this, or for committing to any other practice that resonates with you and serves humanity in the process—sincerely good stuff.

A few more thoughts on centering prayer:

- As I mentioned, the estimated time recommended to spend in prayer is roughly twenty minutes. Using an alarm to keep track of this is totally cool, though not necessary. The more we do this practice, the more our internal alarm clock will know when we've hit twenty minutes (give or take). If you do use an alarm, be sure it isn't one that's loud, as the sounds can completely jolt you out of the experience, which is never a good time.

- If you've eaten, try to wait at least an hour before you do centering prayer. Sitting with a full stomach can cause drowsiness and may result in your falling asleep, which you obviously want to try to avoid. If it happens, it happens. When you wake up, return to your sacred word for a few more minutes before concluding the session. (On the other hand, working with this practice while our stomachs are growling can also be seriously distracting, so eating something light before sitting is fine.)

- The effects of our time spent in prayer will typically be experienced more in our daily lives than during the actual time spent praying. I find it affects me in various ways throughout the day, from unexpected moments of creative inspiration to naturally experiencing a sense of peace and stillness, even while surrounded by a large group of people in environments like concerts or parks. I've even felt the effects while I was at the DMV, and there's something to be said for that!

- Finally, as with any spiritual practice or undertaking, joining a centering prayer group can help you stay committed to your practice, even if you just go once a week. It's like someone who's new to Buddhism finding a sangha for support and guidance, or someone who's new to yoga finding the specific style and teacher that resonates with them and whom they trust to take them deeper into their practice. Support on the path is always a good idea. Don't be shy!

I ask you to believe nothing that
you cannot verify for yourself.

G. I. GURDJIEFF

TRUTH SEEKERS, LOVERS,
AND WARRIORS

ne of my favorite quotes from Ram Dass is, "When you
know how to listen, everybody is the guru speaking to
you. It's right here . . . always."[1] These words have helped me
awaken not only to the wisdom teachings found in sacred texts
and those from illumined teachers, but also those found in the
grittiness of psych wards and rehabs, or in the inspiration of
watching Tony Hawk skate, or Mike Patton take the stage—all
thanks to Everything Mind. Yet it never ceases to amaze me how
uncompromising some people are in their beliefs, *especially* when
it comes to Spirit, God, and religion. Wars over these beliefs are
fought not only on battlefields but also in many of our churches,
meditation centers, synagogues, temples, and more, where the
"our way is the right way" rhetoric is preached by those who
believe they have the definitive answers to life and its mysteries.

I'm not here to add any more fuel to that already-insane fire by claiming that I have the answers myself. Instead, I'd like to relate some of the commonalities we all share not only on our spiritual and/or religious paths, but also in life in general. Because there also are those people who have no interest in formal spirituality or religion, and are still amazing people. They serve humanity in their own way, which some would argue is still "spiritual." But it's all just relative—labels and semantics—so really, who cares what we call it?

Now, I don't want to sound like I'm totally knocking religion, because religion can actually be a valuable container for spiritual experience and community. However, it probably won't come as a shock to many of you reading this that religion—or maybe religious fanaticism would be more applicable—often does more harm than good. It's not only much of the outdated dogmas, or the man-made laws, that stand in the way of progress, but also the way in which many of the worshippers of various religions twist the teachings to fit the mold of whatever works best for their own personal interests, agendas, and gain. Speaking about the unnecessary division many religious practitioners create, the nineteenth-century Indian mystic Sri Ramakrishna said:

> I see people who talk about religion constantly
> quarreling with one another. Hindus, Mussulmans,
> Brahmos, Saktas, Vaishnavas, Saivas all quarrel
> with one another. They haven't the intelligence to
> understand that He who is called Krishna is also Siva
> and the Primal Shakti, and that it is He, again, who is
> called Jesus and Allah. "There is only one Rama and He
> has a thousand names."
>
> Truth is one; only It is called by different names.
> All people are seeking the same Truth; the variance is

due to climate, temperament and name. A lake has many *ghats*. From one *ghat* the Hindus take water in jars and call it *jal*. From another *ghat* the Mussulmans take water in a leather bag and call it *pani*. From a third the Christians take the same thing and call it "water." Suppose someone says that the thing is not *jal* but *pani*, or that it is not *pani* but water, or that it is not water but *jal*. It would indeed be ridiculous. But this very thing is at the root of friction among sects, their misunderstandings and quarrels. This is why people injure and kill one another, and shed blood, in the name of religion. But this is not good. Everyone is going toward God. They will all realize Him if they have sincerity and longing of heart.[2]

As usual, Ramakrishna shares nothing short of tremendous wisdom. Once you have even the slightest taste of the one Rama with a thousand names he speaks about, it becomes undeniable that material and semantic differences are absurd. Again, who really gives a shit what we call our experience of that which is indescribable anyway? If we truly taste it—this completely natural and innocent unity consciousness, this Everything Mind of which we are all a part (regardless of outer appearances, beliefs, opinions, and affiliations)—if even just for a moment, we know that there are no words that can be spoken or written that could even come close to describing It.

Go ahead and call yourself a Christian or atheist, a Hindu, Muslim, Jew, agnostic, Buddhist, or whatever else—there's nothing wrong with any of that. But please don't forget while you're doing so that we're *all* the result of fourteen billion years of evolution, of life's continuing unfolding journey—from atoms to molecules to cells to organisms and *so much more*. We *all* share that. Diversity in life is a beautiful thing, there's no doubt about it, but when we take our differences so seriously, to the point where they cause division and separation, that's where things begin to turn to shit.

In the quote, Ramakrishna also emphasized the point I made earlier about the insanity of people killing one another in the name of religion, which is obviously a direct result of this separation and division. And the only thing crazier than the fact that this is still happening—that people still harm and kill one another in the name of God and religion—is that most of us don't even think twice about it when it's covered on the news. How *insane* is it that as a species we've become completely complacent in accepting this sort of behavior. Seriously, *what the fuck?*

The world, of course, is not all doom and gloom, and there are plenty of shining examples from religious and nonreligious people alike, from those who embody (or have embodied) what the core essence of their particular faith taught, to those who are just kind, compassionate, and service-oriented beings in general with no particular underlying faith as the cause.

There's the amazing heart-centered example set tirelessly by His Holiness the Dalai Lama, who meets joyously with religious and political leaders across the globe, honoring and celebrating their way of life and lineages. There was Saint Teresa of Ávila, a tireless reformer who mentored Saint John of the Cross. Gandhi is also an obvious example of embodied love, as was Christ Jesus. And in a most unexpected turn of events, even the current "punk" (as I like to think of him) Pope Francis, seems to have had enough of the bullshit associated with much of Catholic dogma, citing its excessive focus on gays, abortion, and contraception as "obsessive." In an interview, he was asked what he thought about gay priests, and he replied, "Who am I to judge?"[3] Has hell actually frozen over? Possibly, because on top of that, Pope Francis even invited punk icon Patti Smith to play a Christmas concert at the Vatican. In all fairness, the cynical part of me is waiting for something to give, and for the "too good to be true" pope to reveal his true colors (like Senator Palpatine, who, underneath his nice-guy, clean-cut act, is actually the diabolical Darth Sidious, a.k.a. the Emperor in *Star Wars*), but we'll see.

On the atheist/agnostic/humanist/unitarian side of things, there are people like Noam Chomsky, often called the father of modern linguistics, and one of the most important political activists in recent history. There's David Bohm, one of the most important theoretical physicists of the twentieth century, who spoke out on the dangers of excessive reason and technology, and advocated for authentic and supportive dialogue that he believed could unify conflicting divisions in our social world. Iceland's Björk is celebrated throughout the world, by music fans and critics alike, for her innovative approach to singing and song compositions, as she constantly pushes musical boundaries and provides countless fans with a soundtrack to their own creative lives. R. Buckminster Fuller is celebrated as one of the key innovators of the twentieth century who, among many important contributions to the world, encouraged people to view themselves as passengers on a single-system planet with a common interest in its survival.

Obviously, this list could go on and on, but my hope is that it's becoming clearer (at least for those to whom it wasn't already clear) that there is an inherent goodness in humans regardless of how we identify ourselves on the material level. There is a driving force toward the collective betterment of humanity no matter what we care to call it. Many of us, including myself, use the word *spirituality*, but as we know by now, that is just a word, a concept.

Some people may find spirituality and awakening in a church. Others may experience it through service work, in meditation groups and sanghas, by playing sports, in nature, through martial arts, riding a skateboard, making love, or any combination thereof. (Wait—did I just suggest trying to get it on while skateboarding? Hmm . . .)

Spirituality and the varying paths (again, regardless of whether one chooses to call themselves spiritual or not) are unique to each individual, and at the same time, there's still plenty of similarity. For example, most paths from contemplative Christianity to humanism, and many in between, share an underlying theme of love, compassion, and offering goodwill and kindness toward others. And of course there's the encouragement of practice (and in some traditions devotion) to cultivate deeper wisdom and experience, which, if we're lucky, will lead to transcending any and all differences on the material level as a natural byproduct of Self-realization (or Christ Consciousness, Buddha Mind, Spirit, Stillness, God, ISness, or Being).

Another viewpoint that is very much worth taking into consideration is that of Perennial Philosophy, a philosophical perspective from the fifteenth century. It was championed by the transcendentalists and written about eloquently by Aldous Huxley in his book *The Perennial Philosophy.* The gist of it is that the world's religious traditions share a single and universal truth at their foundation. Huxley offers the following four fundamental doctrines as the core of the philosophy:

First: The phenomenal world of matter and of individualized consciousness—the world of things and animals and men and even gods—is the manifestation of a Divine Ground within which all partial realities have their being, and apart from which they would be nonexistent.

Second: human beings are capable not merely of knowing about the Divine Ground by inference; they can also realize its existence by a direct intuition, superior to discursive reasoning. This immediate knowledge unites the knower with that which is known.

Third: man possesses a double nature, a phenomenal ego and an eternal Self, which is the inner man, the spirit, the spark of divinity within the soul. It is possible for a man, if he so desires, to identify himself with the spirit and therefore with the Divine Ground, which is of the same or like nature with the spirit.

Fourth: man's life on earth has only one end and purpose: to identify himself with his eternal Self and so to come to unitive knowledge of the Divine Ground.[4]

Again, the Divine Ground Huxley speaks about goes by many names. I happen to call it Everything Mind because that's how it's come to make the most sense to me. But whatever word resonates as true for you is great, or if you feel you don't even need a word in the first place, all the better. As we learn to both honor and embrace the similarities on our paths, I believe—no, *I know*—that people can come together in the spirit of unity and greater good for all beings. Isn't that nicer than fighting like schoolchildren over whose path, God, or lack thereof is better? To again quote the wonderful Ramakrishna, "God has made different religions to suit different aspirations, times, and countries. All doctrines are only so many paths; but a path is by no means God Himself. Indeed, one can reach God if one follows any of the paths with whole-hearted devotion."[5]

There is a path that is right for all of us, whether it's traditionally religious, spiritual, or neither. Maybe your path is living in a loft in New York City and staying up each night until three in the morning, painting your heart out while taking periodic breaks for meditation or mindful breathing. Maybe it's moving to India and becoming a renunciant, giving up all worldly possessions in pursuit of truth. Or maybe it's continuing to live as you have been, but with a slightly new outlook on life and a few new techniques and practices that will help you cultivate greater acceptance and compassion for all beings (including yourself).

Whatever you decide, just be real in the process and don't try to over-spiritualize everything. If you're feeling like shit, don't pretend you're not (but don't get wrapped up in a "shit feeling" identity either). If you want to go to a Slayer concert but your "spiritual" friends, or any other friends for that matter, say you shouldn't, honor your own truth and go to a goddamn Slayer concert. Everything in life is part of the spiritual path—part of Everything Mind—and when we live in this awareness, we're bringing spirituality into everything we do.

Life is incredibly strange, and spirituality is incredibly strange, and it all seems to be getting stranger by the minute. So embrace the unknown and explore the shit out of it while you have the chance. In the words of brilliant iconoclast Hunter S. Thompson, "Walk tall. Kick ass. Learn to speak Arabic, love music and never forget you come from a long line of truth seekers, lovers and warriors."[6]

Now get the fuck out there, do amazing things, and make that long line of truth-seekers, lovers, and warriors proud, damn it.

In the spirit of eclectic inspiration and giving credit where credit is due, I offer you the following list of some of the books and albums that kept me inspired while writing *Everything Mind*. May some of them inspire you as well:

Books

Adam Bucko and Matthew Fox, *Occupy Spirituality: A Radical Vision for a New Generation*

Adyashanti, *The End of Your World: Uncensored Straight Talk on the Nature of Enlightenment*

Aldous Huxley, *The Perennial Philosophy: An Interpretation of the Great Mystics, East and West*

Alex Grey, *Net of Being*

Andrew Harvey, *The Direct Path: Creating a Personal Journey to the Divine Using the World's Spiritual Traditions*

Anne Lamott, *Stitches: A Handbook on Meaning, Hope and Repair*

Bo Lozoff, *We're All Doing Time: A Guide for Getting Free*

Brad Warner, *There Is No God and He Is Always with You: A Search for God in Odd Places*

Charles Bukowski, *Love Is a Dog from Hell*

Chris Stedman, *Faithiest: How an Atheist Found Common Ground with the Religious*

Dan Harris, *10% Happier: How I Tamed the Voice in My Head, Reduced Stress Without Losing My Edge, and Found Self-Help That Actually Works—A True Story*

Dana Sawyer, *Huston Smith: Wisdomkeeper: Living the World's Religions: The Authorized Biography of a 21st Century Spiritual Giant*

David Ross Komito, *Nāgārjuna's* Seventy Stanzas: *A Buddhist Psychology Of Emptiness*

don Jose Ruiz and Tami Hudman, *My Good Friend the Rattlesnake: Stories of Loss, Truth, and Transformation*

don Miguel Ruiz Jr., *The Five Levels of Attachment: Toltec Wisdom for the Modern World*

Gen Lamrimpa, *How to Realize Emptiness*

H.P. Lovecraft, *Necronomicon: The Best Weird Tales of H.P. Lovecraft*

His Holiness the Dalai Lama, *Essence of the Heart Sutra: The Dalai Lama's Heart of Wisdom Teachings*

Hunter S. Thompson, *Fear and Loathing on the Campaign Trail '72*

Jarvis Jay Masters, *Finding Freedom: Writings from Death Row*

Jeff Bridges and Bernie Glassman, *The Dude and the Zen Master*

John Dupuy, *Integral Recovery: A Revolutionary Approach to the Treatment of Alcoholism and Addiction*

Jon Wiederhorn and Katherine Turman, *Louder Than Hell: The Definitive Oral History of Metal*

Ken Wilber, *Grace and Grit: Spirituality and Healing in the Life and Death of Treya Killam Wilber* and *The Simple Feeling of Being: Embracing Your True Nature*

Khensur Jampa Tegchok, *Insight into Emptiness*

Maharishi Mahesh Yogi, *Science of Being and Art of Living: Transcendental Meditation*

Matthew Fox, *Meister Eckhart: A Mystic-Warrior for Our Times*

Mirabai Starr, *Caravan of No Despair: A Memoir of Loss and Transformation*

Noah Levine, *Refuge Recovery: A Buddhist Path to Recovering from Addiction*

Pema Chödrön, *When Things Fall Apart: Heart Advice for Difficult Times*

Ram Dass, *Miracle of Love: Stories about Neem Karoli Baba* and *Polishing the Mirror: How to Live from Your Spiritual Heart* (with Rameshwar Das)

Sera Beak, *Red Hot & Holy: A Heretic's Love Story*

Sharon Salzberg, *A Heart as Wide as the World: Stories on the Path of Lovingkindness*

Sri Munagala Venkataramiah, *Talks with Ramana Maharshi*

Swami Prabhavananda and Christopher Isherwood, trans., *Shankara's Crest-Jewel of Discrimination* and *Bhagavad Gita: The Song of God*

Swami Vivekananda, *Jnana-Yoga*

Tara Brach, *Radical Acceptance: Embracing Your Life with the Heart of a Buddha*

Thich Nhat Hanh, *The Diamond That Cuts through Illusion: Commentaries on the Prajnaparamita Diamond Sutra* and *No Death, No Fear: Comforting Wisdom for Life*

Thomas Cleary, *Kensho: The Heart of Zen*

Tommy Rosen, *Recovery 2.0: Move Beyond Addiction and Upgrade Your Life*

Tsem Rinpoche, *Compassion Conquers All: Teachings on the Eight Verses of Mind Transformation*

Tulku Pema Rigtsal, *The Great Secret of Mind: Special Instructions on the Nonduality of Dzogchen*

Venerable Lobsang Gyatso and Tsong Khapa, *The Harmony of Emptiness and Dependent-Arising*

Music

A Tribe Called Quest, *Midnight Marauders*

Anthrax, *Among the Living*

Atmosphere, *Southsiders*

Bear vs. Shark, *Terrorhawk*

Black Sabbath, *Black Sabbath*

Bloodlet, *Entheogen*

Blueprint, *1988*

Burn, *Cleanse*

Cable, *The Failed Convict*

Cannibal Ox, *The Cold Vein*

Cave In, *Until Your Heart Stops*
Cavity, *Supercollider*
Converge, *Petitioning the Empty Sky*
Cursive, *The Ugly Organ*
De La Soul, *Stakes Is High*
Deadguy, *Fixation on a Coworker*
Deafheaven, *Sunbather*
Deltron 3030, *Event 2*
Down, *Down III: Over the Under*
Earth, *Primitive and Deadly*
Empty Flowers, *Four*
Eyehategod, *Eyehategod*
Fucked Up, *David Comes to Life*
Ghostface Killah, *36 Seasons*
Helmet, *Meantime*
High On Fire, *De Vermis Mysteriis*
His Hero Is Gone, *Monuments to Thieves*
Hot Water Music, *Fuel for the Hate Game*
J Mascis, *Tied to a Star*
Jesu, *Everyday I Get Closer to the Light from Which I Came*
Johnny Cash, *Unchained*
Krishna Das, *Kirtan Wallah*
Mogwai, *Rave Tapes*
múm, *Loksins Erum Við Engin*
My Bloody Valentine, *m b v*
Nas, *Illmatic*
Neurosis, *Honor Found in Decay*
Nick Cave & the Bad Seeds, *Push the Sky Away*
Om, *Advaitic Songs*
Overcast, *Reborn to Kill Again*
P.O.S., *Never Better*
Palms, *Palms*
Pelican, *Forever Becoming*
Propagandhi, *Supporting Caste*
Public Enemy, *Fear of a Black Planet*

Queens of the Stone Age, . . . *Like Clockwork*
Quicksand, *Slip*
Red House Painters, *Songs for a Blue Guitar*
Russian Circles, *Memorial*
Scott Kelly, Steve Von Till, Wino, *Songs of Townes Van Zandt*
Shellac, *1000 Hurts*
Sigur Rós, *Takk . . .*
Souls of Mischief, *There Is Only Now*
Sparklehorse, *It's a Wonderful Life*
Suicidal Tendencies, *Lights . . . Camera . . . Revolution!*
Swans, *To Be Kind*
Tears for Fears, *Spotify Session*
The Dillinger Escape Plan, *One of Us Is the Killer*
The Pharcyde, *Bizarre Ride II the Pharcyde*
Today Is the Day, *Animal Mother*
Viktor Vaughn, *Vaudeville Villain*
YOB, *Clearing the Path to Ascend*
Young Widows, *Easy Pain*

NOTES

Introduction

1. Chögyam Trungpa Rinpoche, *The Pocket Chögyam Trungpa* (Boston: Shambhala Publications, 2008), 14.
2. Matthew Fox, *Meditations with Meister Eckhart* (Santa Fe, NM: Bear & Company, 1983), 4.
3. "Das Wesen der Materie" ["The Nature of Matter"], speech in Florence, Italy (1944) (from Archiv zur Geschichte der Max-Planck-Gesellschaft, Abt. Va, Rep. 11 Planck, Nr. 1797).
4. Zach Lind, interview by Chris Grosso, *Mantra Yoga + Health* magazine, 2014, mantramag.com/interview-zach-lind-jimmy-eat-world-chris-grosso/.
5. Chris Stedman, *Faithiest: How an Atheist Found Common Ground with the Religious* (Boston: Beacon Press, 2012), 15.
6. Matthew Fox, *Meister Eckhart: A Mystic-Warrior for Our Times* (Novato, CA: New World Library, 2014), 41.
7. Chögyam Trungpa Rinpoche, *Cutting Through Spiritual Materialism* (Berkeley: Shambhala Publications, 1973), xii.
8. Pema Chödrön, *When Things Fall Apart: Heart Advice for Difficult Times* (Boston: Shambhala Publications, 1997), 110.
9. Father Thomas Keating, interview by Chris Grosso, December 22, 2010, theindiespiritualist.com/2010/12/22/keating/.

Chapter 1: The Goddamn Red Pill

1. Chögyam Trungpa Rinpoche, quoted by Jack Kornfield in interview by Robert Forte, "Psychedelic Experience and Spiritual Practice: A Buddhist Perspective: An Interview with Jack Kornfield," 1986. lycaeum.org/~sputnik/Misc/buddhism.html.
2. Afzal Iqbal, *The Life and Work of Muhammad Jalal-Ud-Din Rumi* (Selangor, Malaysia: The Other Press, 2014), epigraph.

Chapter 3: The Hope and the Hurt

1. "Death Experience," on Sri Ramana Maharshi website, sriramanamaharshi.org/ramana-maharshi/death-experience/.
2. Ken Wilber, *The Pocket Ken Wilber* (Boston: Shambhala Publications, 2008), 90–91.

Chapter 4: Breathe in the Fire

1. "Research FAQs" on Institute of HeartMath website, heartmath.org/support/faqs/research/.
2. Lama Shenpen Drolma, ed., *Change of Heart: The Bodhisattva Peace Training of Chagdud Tulku* (Junction City, CA: Padma Press, 2003), 138.
3. Pema Chödrön, *The Places That Scare You: A Guide to Fearlessness in Difficult Times* (Boston: Shambhala Publications, 2001), 4.
4. Rainer Maria Rilke, *Rilke's Book of Hours: Love Poems to God,* trans. Anita Barrows and Joanna Macy (New York: Riverhead Books, 1996), 119.

Chapter 6: Last Night of the Earth

1. *LIFE* magazine, "The Meaning of Life: The Big Picture," December 1988, 8.
2. Charles Bukowski, *The Last Night of the Earth Poems* (New York: HarperCollins/Ecco, 2002), 120–121.

Chapter 7: Blood, Broken Bones, Violence, and Other Joys of Meditation

1. Brad Warner, *Hardcore Zen: Punk Rock, Monster Movies & the Truth about Reality* (Somerville, MA: Wisdom Publications, 2003), 198.

Chapter 9: Death in the Air

1. Ken Wilber, *The Integral Vision: A Very Short Introduction to the Revolutionary Integral Approach to Life, God, the Universe, and Everything* (Boston: Shambhala Publications, 2007), 187.

Practice: Shadow Self

1. Ken Wilber, *The Integral Vision,* 191.

Chapter 12: The Chemistry of Common Life

1. don Miguel Ruiz, *The Four Agreements: A Practical Guide to Personal Freedom* (San Rafael, CA: Amber-Allen Publishing, 1997), 48–49.

Chapter 14: Mastodon, King Kong, and Inspiration

1. Brann Dailor of Mastodon, interview by Chris Grosso for Suicide Girls website, July 23, 2013, suicidegirls.com/girls/jessxdavis/blog/2680488/mastodon/.
2. Ibid.

Chapter 15: In All the Worlds until the End of Time

1. Ken Wilber, *The Integral Vision,* 222–223.
2. Ibid.

Chapter 16: Love. Serve. Remember.

1. Ram Dass, *Polishing the Mirror: How to Live From Your Spiritual Heart* (Boulder, CO: Sounds True, 2013) 52.
2. Andrew Harvey, *The Hope: A Guide To Sacred Activism* (Carlsbad, CA: Hay House, 2009), 13.
3. Kabir, *Kabir: Ecstatic Poems*, trans. Robert Bly (Boston: Beacon Press, 2004). Reprinted with permission.

Chapter 17: We Are the Storm

1. Alison Luterman, "What We Came For," *The Sun,* Issue 250, October 1996, thesunmagazine.org/issues/250/ what_we_came_for?page=2.
2. Neil deGrasse Tyson, *The Universe,* Season 1, Episode 14: "The Big Bang," televised on The History Channel, 2007.

Practice: Inner Body Awareness

1. Eckhart Tolle, *Oneness With All Life: Inspired Selections from A New Earth* (New York: Penguin Group, 2009), 148.

Chapter 18: In Pieces

1. Thich Nhat Hanh, *Awakening of the Heart: Essential Buddhist Sutras and Commentaries* (Berkeley, CA: Parallax Press, 2012), 421.
2. The Dalai Lama, *The Essence of the Heart Sutra: The Dalai Lama's Heart of Wisdom Teachings,* trans. and ed. Geshe Thupten Jinpa (Somerville, MA: Wisdom Publications, 2002), 30.
3. John Daido Loori, *Zen Mountain Monastery Liturgy Manual* (Mt. Tremper, NY: Dharma Communications, 1998), 27–28.
4. Thich Nhat Hanh, *Your True Home: The Everyday Wisdom of Thich Nhat Hanh* (Boston: Shambhala Publications, 2011), 195.

Practice: The Five Remembrances

1. Thich Nhat Hanh, *The Heart of the Buddha's Teaching: Transforming Suffering into Peace, Joy, and Liberation* (New York: Broadway Books, 1999), 124.

Chapter 19: The "End of My Rope" Is a Noose

1. Jeff Bridges and Bernie Glassman, *The Dude and the Zen Master* (New York: Blue Rider Press, 2012), 29.

Chapter 20: At the Mountain of Madness

1. Barry Magid, *Ending the Pursuit of Happiness: A Zen Guide* (Somerville, MA: Wisdom Publications, 2008), xiii.

2. Dilgo Khyentse Rinpoche, *The Hundred Verses of Advice: Tibetan Buddhist Teachings on What Matters Most* (Boston: Shambhala Publications, 2002), 106.

Practice: Die, Die, My Darling

1. J. Krishnamurti, television interview by Ross Saunders, Sydney, Australia, November 1970, youtube.com/watch?v=YAJjAuRl0Qc.
2. Kahlil Gibran, *The Prophet* (New York: Borzoi Books, 1951), 81.

Chapter 21: No Apologies

1. Andrew Harvey, Adam Bucko, and Chris Grosso, "Finding Your Own Path," for SynchCast website, December 2014, synchcast. net/#!finding-your-own-path/c1zdh.
2. Ibid.
3. *Talking Leaves: A Journal of Spiritual Ecology/Activism*, Volumes 10–12 (Deep Ecology Education Project, 2000), 20.

Chapter 23: On Suffering (And How to Fit the Entire Human Race into a Single Sugar Cube)

1. Ram Dass, *One Liners: A Mini-Manual for a Spiritual Life* (New York: Bell Tower Publishing, 2002), 79.
2. Marcus Chown, "Top 4 Bonkers Things about the Universe," Physics.org, physics.org/featuredetail.asp?id=41.

Practice: One with the Eternal Everything (Guided Meditation)

1. Ram Dass, *Polishing the Mirror*, 9.

Chapter 24: Bleed Into One

1. Tara Brach, *Radical Acceptance: Embracing Your Life with the Heart of a Buddha* (New York: Bantam Books, 2003), 73.

Practice: Maranatha Mantra

1. Andrew Harvey, *Son of Man: The Mystical Path to Christ* (New York: Jeremy P. Tarcher/Putnam, 1998), 202.

Practice: Centering Prayer

1. Father Thomas Keating, *Open Mind, Open Heart: The Contemplative Dimension of the Gospel* (New York: Continuum, 2006), 138.
2. Father Thomas Keating, "The Method of Centering Prayer," on Contemplative Outreach website, contemplativeoutreach.org/category/category/centering-prayer.

Chapter 26: Truth Seekers, Lovers, and Warriors

1. Ram Dass, *Be Here Now* (Hanuman Foundation, 1978), 78.
2. Andrew Harvey, *The Essential Mystics: The Soul's Journey into Truth* (New York: HarperCollins, 1996), 53.
3. "Pope Francis on Gays: Who Am I To Judge?" article on Huffington Post website, July 29, 2013, huffingtonpost.com/2013/07/29/pope-francis-gays_n_3669635.html.
4. Aldous Huxley, introduction to *Bhagavad-Gita: The Song of God,* trans. Swami Prabhavananda and Christopher Isherwood (Hollywood, CA: Vedanta Press, 1987), 7.
5. Ramakrishna, quoted by Huston Smith in *The Illustrated World's Religions: A Guide to Our Wisdom Traditions* (New York: HarperOne, 1995), 56.
6. William McKeen, *Outlaw Journalist: The Life and Times of Hunter S. Thompson* (New York: W. W. Norton & Company, 2009), 350.

ACKNOWLEDGMENTS

I'd like to humbly offer my deepest gratitude for all the love and support throughout the process of writing this book to: Jenn Grosso and Morgan "Momo" Walker; Brenda and Lawrence Grosso; Jay, Catie, and Addison Grosso; Peter and Francine Lui; Allison Lui and Will Campbell; Scott Walker; Ken Wilber; Michele Martin and Steve Harris; Nancy Smith; Jennifer Brown, Alice Peck, Haven Iverson, Tami Simon, and the rest of my family at Sounds True; Justin Mehl; Lisa Braun Dubbels; Jill Angelo-Birnbaum; Dana Sawyer; Sera Beak; Adam Bucko; Tanya Lee Markul, Andréa Balt and *Rebelle Society;* Jarvis Jay Masters and Kathrin Smith; Jessica Durivage-Kerridge; Betsy Chasse; Miguel Ruiz, Jr.; Jose Ruiz and Tami Hudman; Lissa Rankin; Ram Dass; Raghu Markus; David Silver; Rachael Fisher; Noah Lampert; Mirabai Starr; Tommy Rosen; Corey DeVos; Jen Taylor, Justin Good and The Sanctuary at Shepardfields; Valerie Gangas; Tracy McCormick; Maranda Pleasant; Kate Bartolotta; Sharon Pingitore; Eben Sterling; Karina MacKenzie; Deron Drumm, Kelvin Young, Hilary Bryant, and everyone at Toivo by Advocacy Unlimited; Breeze Floyd and Love Resembles; Ron Tannebaum, Ken Pomerance and InTheRooms.com; Bernie Romanowski; Darrell Tauro; Amy Scher; Michele Ignatowicz; Jessica Pimentel; Keli Lalita; Jamison Monroe and Newport Academy; Miguel Chen; Steven Farina; Chelsea Genzano; Jonas Elrod; Alanna Kaivalya; Jennifer Colon; Kayla de Both, George

Beecher, Gary Sanders, Sarit Rogers, Noah Levine and all my Dharma Punx/Against The Stream family; J.P. Sears and Diana Deaver; Chris and Leigh Burton; Nyk Danu; Deanna Ogle; and Chris Stedman. And to all the other amazing people not listed here who've supported me along the way, please know that your name is sincerely written on my heart in gratitude.

ABOUT THE AUTHOR

Chris Grosso is a public speaker, writer, recovering addict, spiritual director, and author of *Indie Spiritualist: A No Bullshit Exploration of Spirituality*. He writes for *ORIGIN* magazine, *Huffington Post*, and *Mantra Yoga + Health* magazine, and has spoken and performed at Wanderlust Festival, *Yoga Journal* Conference, Sedona World Wisdom Days, Kripalu, and more. He hosts The Indie Spiritualist podcast on the Mindpod Network. A self-taught musician, Chris has been writing, recording, and touring since the mid-90s.

He is passionate about his work with people who are in the process of healing or struggling with addictions of all kinds. He speaks and leads groups in detoxes, yoga studios, rehabs, youth centers, 12-step meetings, hospitals, conferences, and festivals worldwide. He is a member of the advisory board for Drugs over Dinner.

Learn more about Chris at his website: theindiespiritualist.com.

ABOUT SOUNDS TRUE

Sounds True is a multimedia publisher whose mission is to inspire and support personal transformation and spiritual awakening. Founded in 1985 and located in Boulder, Colorado, we work with many of the leading spiritual teachers, thinkers, healers, and visionary artists of our time. We strive with every title to preserve the essential "living wisdom" of the author or artist. It is our goal to create products that not only provide information to a reader or listener, but that also embody the quality of a wisdom transmission.

For those seeking genuine transformation, Sounds True is your trusted partner. At SoundsTrue.com you will find a wealth of free resources to support your journey, including exclusive weekly audio interviews, free downloads, interactive learning tools, and other special savings on all our titles.

To learn more, please visit SoundsTrue.com/freegifts or call us toll free at 800-333-9185.